Charles Buchan's
MANCHESTER UNITED GIFT BOOK

selections from

CHARLES BUCHAN'S PUBLICATIONS

1951-73

Dear Reader,

As this is the first Gift Book which I have edited for you, I would like to begin this little introduction by saying how much I hope you will enjoy the stories and pictures which have been gathered together for you.

I expect many of you who are reading this are already old friends of mine, boys who keep in touch with our greatest game through the columns of "Football Monthly". But, whether we have already met, or whether we are meeting here for the first time, I welcome you all, knowing how keen you are on sport and how sound is your judgement.

Now it is your judgement that can help me. Let me know if you enjoy this book - and if you do like it, tell your pals about it.

If, on the other hand, you have criticisms to make, let me know of them and you can be sure I will do my very best to carry out your suggestions when we publish this book in future years.

The idea has been to give you variety, to provide exciting reading, and to print pictures which will capture highlights of the game and the great footballers who make it so popular with us all.

I believe the recipe will be to your liking and hope that when you have finished this volume you will begin to look forward to next year's!

**Charles Buchan's introduction
to his first Soccer Gift Book, 1953–1954**

Charles Buchan's Manchester United Gift Book
© Malavan Media and Football Monthly Ltd 2007

Malavan Media is a creative consultancy responsible
for the Played in Britain series of books and events
www.playedinbritain.co.uk

Edited by Simon Inglis
Text by Mark Wylie and Simon Inglis
Design by Doug Cheeseman and Jörn Kröger
Production by Jackie Spreckley
ISBN: 978 0 9547445 4 0
Printed by Zrinski, Croatia

Charles Buchan's

MANCHESTER UNITED GIFT BOOK

Edited by
Simon Inglis

Introduction by
Mark Wylie

Published by Malavan Media

Cont

ents

TALKING IT OVER ... by JOHN THOMPSON

From the beginning...

AT first there was one chair in the office of "Football Monthly." I cannot remember why. We were hard-up for furniture for a long time. We would take it in turns to perch round a trestle table on orange boxes and would courteously leave the chair for any visitor who proved himself healthy enough to climb the steep stairs leading to our new home.

The trestle table was covered with a grey blanket and smelled of old apples. This was probably because Covent Garden was just round the corner.

Long before "Football Monthly" increased its tangible assets in any substantial way, Charles Buchan climbed the stairs with a purchase wrapped in brown paper. It was a splendidly expensive feather-duster.

Every morning Charles would whisk it energetically over the walls, the little pieces of furniture and the weary strips of linoleum.

Then he would look around as proudly as if he had just scored the winning goal against Scotland.

The moment he had finished, all the dust would settle down gracefully to await the next disturbance. The office overlooked the Strand, London . . . buses almost passed through the room, and it was difficult to keep clean for any time at all.

That first winter was singularly comfortless. In an unenviable spot, furthest from the windows, Joe Sarl would peer with a kind of hopeless determination at typescript and proofs and emerge at the end of the day with the lost look of a man who has been wandering through a thick fog.

He was, however, the warmest of our company.

To avoid frost-bite from the draughts that whistled through the room, Charles Buchan would wrap newspapers round his legs. The paper rustled disconcertingly whenever he moved.

LONG before winter fell, there had been the task of reading the first contributions to our first issue. There had been a fascinating incongruity in sitting on an orange box and studying the earliest article to arrive.

It came from that fine and kindly friend, the Marquess of Londonderry. He had been converted to Soccer by his friendship with miners in his father's pits.

There was a certain dream-like quality in reading Lord Londonderry's description of how he had become a director of Arsenal . . . because of a conversation over dinner at Buckingham Palace with the Master of the Horse, who happened to be Chairman of Arsenal.

Well, Buckingham Palace was only down the road from our office. And for a moment the bare electric light bulb was a candelabrum . . .

As this one hundredth edition of "Football Monthly" was being prepared, I glanced with nostalgia through that long-ago Number One.

The front cover picture was of Stanley Matthews, of Blackpool and England. **There could be no other choice, for Matthews has enriched the pleasures of us all and, in the years that have intervened, there has been no challenger for his place among the giants.**

Inside, were pictures of little Henry Cockburn, of Manchester United, and of Jimmy Dickinson, who has served Portsmouth with devoted loyalty through so many triumphs and disasters.

There, too, were bow-legged Joe Mercer and Mal Griffiths, the happy Welshman, and George Young leading out Scotland, and Jimmy Mason poised over the ball in the colours of Third Lanark. All were players remembered now with gratitude.

There, too, was Joe Harvey, telling with humility of the day Newcastle United won the F.A. Cup . . . *The King handed it to me and as he did so, I had the feeling that all the good people of Tyneside were with me . . . I felt that His Majesty was giving the Cup to me not as Joe Harvey, but as the representative of all those supporters, that I was getting it on their behalf.*

The Queen gave me my medal and I made my way down the steps, perhaps stumbling a little because I was near to tears . . .

TURN again the yellowing pages of that old "Football Monthly". Here is Raich Carter talking of bomb-battered Hull . . . *It was the success of Hull City Soccer team that helped to put Hull back on the map and restore the morale of people who had come to regard themselves as isolated and forgotten . . .*

Arthur Drewry, then Chairman of England's Selectors, told how *his imagination had been fired in Argentina and Brazil by the development of football grounds as first-class social centres; the centre-piece of the local community for every kind of recreative sport . . .*

Turn the pages . . . here is J. B. Priestley, capturing, as he did so well in "The Good Companions", the emotions of those who follow our greatest game . . . *It turned you into a member of a new community, all brothers together for an hour-and-a-half, for not only had you escaped from the clanking machinery of this less life, from work, wages, rent, doles, sick pay, insurance cards, nagging wives, ailing children, bad bosses, idle workmen, but you had escaped with most of your neighbours, with half the town, and there you were, cheering together, thumping one another on the shoulders, swopping judgments like lords of the earth, having pushed your way through a turnstile into another and altogether more splendid kind of life, hurtling with Conflict and yet passionate and beautiful in its Art . . .*

AND now, close the pages and consider for a moment how "Football Monthly" grew from its orange-box days into the voice of the greatest game man ever played, the game that spans frontiers with a handshake and knows no barriers of race or belief.

"Football Monthly" became a unique 'family affair'. Readers sent ideas and views on how to improve the magazine. Never had a publication received such friendly and loyal support.

The family was scattered, as the magic of football is scattered.

There was a boy in Brazil, a shoe-maker in Alaska, a judge's son in Yugoslavia, the skipper of a tug-boat who took two copies so that he could send one to an unknown kid in hospital.

There was a cinema manager in Australia, a cipher clerk in a British Embassy, a lance-corporal in the Malayan jungle.

The addresses from which they wrote ranged from Bolton to Burma. They came from destroyers and trawlers, factories and farms. Some were at village schools, others at Eton.

Thus did "Football Monthly" prosper because of the kindliness and understanding of its readers.

And it is the kindliness that will be remembered always— the gifts that readers asked us to send to sick children at Christmas, the gestures that helped old players down on their luck.

There were letters from prisons and mansions and there was the miracle of finding how blind people retain their love for football.

And the family grew and gained in strength and influence. It is loyal and sturdy, as it always was. We are very proud of it . . .

▲ December 1959

Foreword

by Simon Inglis
Played in Britain series editor

For the discerning football fan of the 1950s and 1960s, *Charles Buchan's Football Monthly* was an absolute essential. If not for reading, then for the supply of bedroom posters.

Of course there were other publications on the market, such as the weekly *Sport* magazine, which ran until 1957, or *Soccer Star*, established in 1952. But neither had such bold design, such vibrant colour images, the collectability, the satisfying weightiness, nor any of the cameraderie that Charles Buchan and his team so knowingly infused into the pages of *Football Monthly*.

To be a reader of Charlie's magazine was to be a member of a fraternity.

In the world of Charles Buchan – a former Sunderland and Arsenal player known to millions for his match reports on BBC Radio – football was Soccer (always with a capital S), and Soccer was 'grand'. Indeed most things in Charlie's world were grand. The players were grand, the matches were grand, the footballing life itself was grand.

Buchan's magazine first appeared in September 1951 (when Charlie was already aged 61), just as the Festival of Britain was winding down on London's South Bank. Rationing was still in place. Paper was still in short supply. National Service was still obligatory for young men, while thousands of British troops were serving in Korea.

In the six years since Hitler's defeat, attendance levels at English football had soared to record levels, topping 41 million in 1948–49. Yet never before had the fortunes of the national team been so low, following England's humiliating defeat by the USA during the 1950 World Cup in Brazil (a match witnessed by Buchan and several of the Fleet Street veterans who would become his regular contributors).

Thus hope for the future, in the bright new world of post-war Britain, was necessarily tempered by anxiety concerning the health of the national game. Similarly, parochial pride in our footballing greats had always to be counterbalanced by reluctant admiration for the obvious skills of those 'Continentals' and 'Latins' from overseas. Hot-headed and devious they may have been, but clearly they had much to teach us, about tactics, training, even what kind of boots to wear.

So successful was *Charles Buchan's Football Monthly* that in July 1953 the publishers issued the first *Charles Buchan's Soccer Gift Book*. For the next two decades this jaunty annual earned an automatic slot on the Christmas wish lists of thousands of schoolboys.

Buchan himself, despite his reporting commitments with the BBC and the *News Chronicle* – whose staff he had joined in 1928 after retiring from Arsenal – remained actively involved in both publications until his death in June 1960, while on holiday in Monte Carlo. He was a tall man, always immaculately dressed and unfailingly polite. Columnist John Macadam, another writer of the old school, said of him, 'Charles sees only the good in all men.' But whereas Macadam and several of his fellow writers were hard drinking adventurers, Buchan retained the image of a schoolmasterly gent. And yet in his prime he had been both a supremely gifted and wily inside forward – his ratio of 224 goals in 413 games for Sunderland still stands as a record – and a brave soldier, winning a Military Cross during the First World War (a fact he modestly omitted from his autobiography, published in 1955).

By 1958 *Football Monthly's* circulation had risen to 107,000, at which point the offices moved from the Strand to 161-166 Fleet Street.

By a curious coincidence, this was the site of Andertons Hotel, where the Football League had formed in 1888. Not only that but the new building, Hulton House, was owned by the former publishers of *Athletic News*, once Britain's most popular football weekly.

After Charlie's death the proprietors kept his name on the masthead (until 1971), and under new editor Pat Collins – buoyed up by England's World Cup victory in 1966 – increased circulation to 200,000 in 1968. The following year it reached an all-time peak of 254,000. Membership of the Boys' Club topped 100,000.

Changing fashions may explain part of the magazine's demise in the early 1970s. As hairstyles lengthened and trousers grew more flared, more young readers were veering away from programme and autograph swaps in favour of records and pop-related memorabilia. Football itself was entering a period of decline, as the ravages of hooliganism began to take their toll on attendances.

Charlie's seemingly more innocent world was fading rapidly.

But also crucial was the decision by *Football Monthly's* new holding company, Longacre Press, to publish a sister magazine called *Goal*, in 1968. It took two years for *Goal* to outsell *Football Monthly*. Then a third contender materialised in the form of *Shoot*, a brash new weekly, published by IPC.

Shoot and *Goal* each sold over 220,000 copies weekly in 1971, compared with 164,000, and falling, for *Football Monthly*.

In August 1973 the publishers responded by rebranding the title in a smaller format. But as editor Pat Collins suspected, it was a losing battle, and in August 1974 the title left Fleet Street and became *Football Magazine*.

A golden era had truly passed.

'**Our object is to provide a publication that will be worthy of our National game and the grand sportsmen who play and watch it.**'

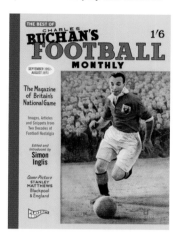

The compilation which follows is selected from issues of *Charles Buchan's Football Monthly* dating 1951–73, and from the *Charles Buchan's Soccer Gift Books*, published annually from 1953–74.

Inevitably readers will spot gaps; star players unmentioned, key events uncovered. Some of these omissions arise from lack of space. Others are simply owing to the fact that the magazine and gift books were by no means comprehensive in their coverage. If there is a narrative in what follows, therefore, it is fractured rather than cohesive, though hopefully no less appealing when viewed as a whole.

It will be noted that this book forms part of *Played in Britain*, a series which seeks to celebrate and preserve these islands' extraordinary sporting heritage.

Heritage is generally thought to reside in historic buildings, in places and landscapes. What it is hoped the following pages demonstrate is that there is heritage in ephemera too, and in the shared narrative that make us a nation, and a footballing nation at that.

For more on the Charles Buchan archive, see our list of related publications on the back page.

DENNIS VIOLLET (Manchester United)

Manchester United 1951–73

by Mark Wylie
Curator of the Manchester United Museum at Old Trafford

Every football club goes through its highs and lows, so it was only by pure chance that the years in which *Charles Buchan's Football Monthly* and his *Soccer Gift Books* were in production, from 1951–74, should coincide with two of the most remarkable decades in the history of Manchester United.

But a fortunate coincidence it was too, for were the tales of triumph and tribulation experienced by United during this extraordinary period to be translated into a work of fiction, most readers would dismiss the plot as pure fantasy.

Yet there is no need to embellish the truth. Life at Old Trafford – from the club's revival in the immediate post-war years until its relegation in 1974, coloured as it was by the events of 1958 and 1968, and by a cavalcade of such vivid characters and personal stories – forms an integral part of the narrative of 20th century popular culture in Britain.

For sure numerous histories of the club have covered this period in detail, and many readers will not need reminding of the salient facts. But this compilation of articles and images from the Charles Buchan archive undoubtedly adds a lively and evocative dimension to the story, providing snapshots of how the club's image developed, how its stars were portrayed to a generation of fans, and how the foundation of the club's current status found its roots in the popular imagination.

Today, of course, United are one of the world's richest, most famous sporting clubs. Yet this immense wealth and international repute is a relatively new phenomenon.

Apart from one brief period of glory under Ernest Mangnall prior to 1914 – when two League titles and the FA Cup were won – until the late 1940s United's story was largely one of under-achievement.

Gates mostly fluctuated between 20-30,000. The club was usually in debt, and for years was not even the dominant force in Manchester. For most of the 1920s and 1930s Old Trafford, the 80,000 capacity stadium built with such high hopes in 1910, took on a forlorn air.

In 1931, by which point gates had fallen below 12,000, United had even to be rescued from bankruptcy by businessman James Gibson, while two seasons later the team was one match away from the ignominy of Third Division football.

Small wonder that United were the butt of music hall comedians.

Yet by the end of the decade came signs of recovery. After the departure of manager Scott Duncan in 1937, a committee led by secretary Walter Crickmer took over team affairs, and in 1938 United were back in the First Division. A year later Old Trafford witnessed a record crowd of nearly 77,000.

But then came the war, and in March 1941 German bombers – aiming to destroy the manufacturing capacity of the adjoining Trafford Park industrial estate – laid waste to Old Trafford's main stand, forcing United to move to neighbours Manchester City and plummeting the club further into debt.

Enter, at this crucial juncture, the man who was to become the embodiment of Manchester United in the post war era and beyond.

Born in the tough, working class environs of Scotland's Lanarkshire coalfields and raised as a strict Catholic, Matt Busby had considered emigrating to Canada, until in 1928 his footballing skills caught the attention of Manchester City. There he carved a successful career as an attacking wing half, before moving to Liverpool in 1936.

After spending the war years as an army physical training instructor, Busby had the chance to return to Anfield as a coach, but instead he preferred to accept United's invitation to assume the more senior managerial role at Old Trafford, a post he took up in October 1945.

With United some £15,000 in debt and still sharing at Maine Road, his was a baptism of fire.

Then aged 36, he was hardly older than several of the players he inherited from United's pre-war side. Yet it proved a blessing to have such a nucleus of seasoned professionals at his disposal.

Shrewdly Busby identified their strengths and weaknesses. Dubliner Johnny Carey, for example, moved from inside forward to become one of United's greatest full-backs and captains. Carey was also voted Player of the Year in 1949, an award that Charles Buchan had helped initiate the previous year.

Jack Rowley moved from outside-left to become a phenomenal centre-forward, while the defence was built around the towering Allenby Chilton, a Normandy veteran who had made his debut in United's last match before the outbreak of war in 1939.

Remarkably United finished as First Division runners-up four times in Busby's first five seasons. Just as importantly, in 1948 United overcame a Stanley Matthews inspired Blackpool to win the 1948 Cup Final at Wembley, the club's first Cup triumph since 1909. At the time, with Old Trafford still a wreck, the club did not even have a trophy cabinet.

Matters off the field soon improved however. So high had been United's gates at Maine Road – hitting an all-time League record of 83,260 v. Arsenal in January 1948 – that City, although grateful for the rent, asked them to leave. Finally, after months of lobbying for the necessary steel permits, reconstruction commenced at Old Trafford in 1949, allowing United to return after eight homeless years.

So it was that by the time the first edition of *Charles Buchan's Football Monthly* hit the bookstands in September 1951, United were regarded as one of the major forces in English football, a reputation they sealed by winning their first League title since 1911, at the end of the magazine's first season in print.

Manchester during this period was far from the modern metropolis we know today. Renowned for its rainfall, the city suffered additionally from smog and pollution. Rationing was still the norm, poverty was rife, bomb damage from the war was still widespread, and adequate housing remained in short supply.

But employment levels at least remained high, particularly in and around Trafford Park and the Manchester Docks, where industry had been quick to adapt to post-war needs and where decline would not set in until the mid 1960s.

For Manchester United's players a taste of what lay beyond austerity Britain came with tours to the United States in both 1950 and 1952. The USA, it will be recalled, had against all the odds beaten England during the 1950 World Cup. But the tours also had unintended consequences.

On meeting members of the United party, American baseball players expressed their amazement that British footballers were subject to a maximum wage, and a low one at that. (It went up from £12 to £14 a week in June 1951.)

For winger Charlie Mitten, the lure of greater riches saw him jump ship and join the Colombian club, Santa Fé of Bogotá.

His move caused an uproar in Manchester, and although Mitten returned after a year, Busby suspended him for six months before selling him to Fulham. (Busby had already flexed his disciplinary muscle two years earlier by selling Johnny Morris to Derby, after a series of disagreements.) ▶

◀ September 1957

Concerned that his squad was now ageing Busby's attentions next switched to youth.

United's youth policy had in fact been set up in 1938 by chairman James Gibson. The aim had been to create a team of local players, so that cash strapped United would incur less expense on transfer fees.

Now, aided by Busby's friend and assistant, Jimmy Murphy, together with coaches Bert Whalley, Tom Curry and Bill Inglis, and by a widening network of scouts led by Joe Armstrong, United sought to extend this remit by bringing in schoolboys from across the country. Not only that but United entered their juniors into open-age competitions against local 'works' teams, so that the boys were thrown into action against men.

Toughened by their experiences in these games, United's rampant youngsters went on to win the FA Youth Cup five years in succession.

Not only did 'the Busby Babes' (or 'Golden Apples' as Jimmy Murphy preferred) challenge the accepted notion that a successful team could only ever field two or three youngsters, but the likes of Mark Jones, Duncan Edwards, Jackie Blanchflower, Jeff Whitefoot and Bill Foulkes also lent United an air of glamour, at just the time British youth was evolving its own, quite separate social identity. As the photograph of David Pegg, Colin Webster and Tommy Taylor on page 27 indicates, with their American-style quiffs, T-shirts and casual wear, here were the proto-typical footballers of the rock 'n roll age.

Inevitably this rich store of talent provoked envious comments from rivals. But it was not long before other clubs followed suit. Charles Buchan himself applauded this trend. After England's humiliating defeats by Hungary in 1953 and 1954, clearly something had to be done to revive the national game.

One factor that United were often at pains to point out, to the press and to intending apprentices, was the family atmosphere prevailing both at Old Trafford and at The Cliff, the club's training ground in Salford (purchased in 1938). At United, it was stressed, all the stars pulled together for the good of the team.

In its own way, *Football Monthly*, with its cheery photo spreads and mostly uncritical reports, helped to reinforce this impression.

But football was still some years away from recasting its image altogether. However much Busby argued that the modern player was better off than his predecessors, the maximum wage still meant that footballers remained firmly rooted within their communities. Few could afford cars. Many still travelled to Old Trafford on the bus from their lodgings or from their modest rented club houses, mingling with fans before and after games.

Several were plagued by self-doubt. Competition was fierce. Inevitably the majority of youngsters failed to make the grade, and in some cases were never heard of again, having had their photographs featured in the magazine. There was also the worry that a call up for National Service could severely dent one's chances (and even one's fitness, if some managers were to be believed).

That said, *Football Monthly* interviews invariably concluded with the message that by putting in extra effort and listening to advice, self belief would return and success would eventually be earned.

Not all this was soft propaganda. A genuine camaraderie did exist at Old Trafford during this period. In the Babes' first title-winning season of 1955-56, only Johnny Berry and Roger Byrne, the team captain and father figure, were over 25.

Blooded in the FA Youth Cup, then crowned by a further League title in 1956, Busby's Babes were next to achieve even greater renown as pioneers in Europe.

The idea for a European club tournament originated with the French football magazine *L'Equipe*, and was made possible by the increasing use of floodlights for mid-week matches and by the greater availability of air travel. (It was no coincidence that British European Airways started advertising in *Football Monthly* around this time, as shown on page 37.)

Chelsea, as League champions in 1955, were the first English club invited to enter the tournament, but their chairman, Joe Mears, was quickly pressured into withdrawing by the Football League Management Committee. European matches, its members argued with characteristic conservatism, offered a direct threat to domestic fixtures and to attendances. In contrast the Scottish club Hibernian were happy to take up their invitation and progressed very creditably to the inaugural competition's semi-finals.

For Matt Busby there could be no doubt. After the two debacles against Hungary, English football had to adapt to the style of football being developed overseas, and as League champions in 1956, he felt it was up to United to pave the way. Fortunately his hard working chairman, Harold Hardman, agreed, seeing the benefits not only of enhancing United's international reputation but also of earning the vital extra income needed to improve Old Trafford (which still had comparatively few seats or terrace cover, and no floodlights).

For the League's hierarchy, United's stance represented open defiance but, after a series of spectacular results in their debut European season, ending only with defeat in the semi-finals in 1957, it was the players themselves who did most to justify Busby's resolve.

Moreover, popular opinion now swung behind United. Already the Busby Babes were the team that fans flocked to see in domestic games. Now they were carrying the torch into Europe.

Charles Buchan, who from the magazine's beginning had praised the footballing prowess of other nations, also took up the European cause. In April 1957 (see page 32) he even urged the inclusion of Russian clubs, at a time when the Cold War was getting ever colder.

A further factor in spreading the European creed was the fact that several matches were covered by television, at a time when television ownership was increasing massively throughout Britain. (Manchester played a key part in this expansion as home to the new commercial station, Granada, launched in 1956 from the country's first purpose-built television studios, on Quay Street.) For the first time British viewers were now able to see how foreign clubs played, what style shirts they wore, and how skimpy were their modern boots.

It proved an intoxicating draw.

But for all their early success, United could ill afford to rattle the ultra-sensitive officials at the Football League.

As is indelibly imprinted upon the memories of all fans from this period, on Saturday, February 1 1958, United won an epic First Division match at Highbury, beating Arsenal 5-4 (a match Buchan described as one of most wonderful exhibitions he had seen for years).

The following Wednesday, fielding the same line-up, United recorded a 3-3 draw in the second leg of their European Cup tie against Red Star, in Belgrade. For the second season in succession, a place in the competition's semi-finals beckoned.

The next morning, conscious that the team had to get back to Manchester as soon as possible

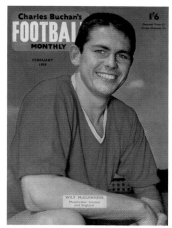

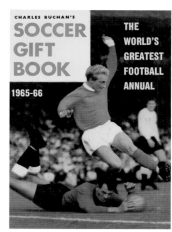

▲ February 1959

▲ 1965–66 Gift Book

to prepare for Saturday's League game against Wolves, the journey home began, taking in what should have been a brief refuelling stop at Munich-Reim airport. Weather conditions there were appalling, but United had to get back, and after two aborted attempts to take off, the BEA airliner made its final, fateful attempt at 3.04pm.

Thus on the snow and ice of the Munich runway, the dreams and hopes of England's first European pioneers came to a shattering end.

United, champions twice in 1956 and 1957, and FA Cup runners-up in 1957, were left mourning the greatest disaster ever to befall an English club.

Seven players, their average age 24, died at the scene: chirpy Eddie Colman, who appeared on the cover of the December 1957 issue (page 41), Tommy Taylor, featured living it up in Madrid in September 1957 (page 40), Liam 'Bill' Whelan, pictured in October 1957 (page 39), Roger Byrne, selected as *Star of the Season* the year before (page 37), Mark Jones, interviewed in January 1957 (page 30), Dave Pegg, seen in the 1955–56 Gift Book (page 27) and Geoff Bent, from Salford.

Most poignantly of all, the March 1958 edition of *Football Monthly*, prepared just days before the disaster, featured Duncan Edwards on its cover.

Edwards, 21 years old and widely regarded as the finest of his generation, and certainly as a future England captain, was still alive when taken from the crash, but died in a Munich hospital fifteen days later, on February 21. By cruel fate, this was almost exactly the same day that the magazine went on sale.

A black bordered slip of paper, hurriedly inserted into each issue (reproduced on page 45), provides eloquent testament to the national sense of grief.

United's loss was also England's. Taylor, Byrne and Edwards were all seasoned internationals. Had they survived, might England's chances have been improved in the 1958 World Cup? Given that Edwards would have been aged only 29 in 1966, might even the World Cup eleven have lined up differently?

Also killed at Munich were three United officials, secretary Walter Crickmer, chief coach Bert Whalley and trainer Tom Curry, while amongst the other twelve fatalities were eight journalists, most of them Manchester-based, including the *News of the World* reporter, Frank Swift, a former England and Manchester City goalkeeper. All these pressmen would have been known to staff on *Football Monthly*, and particularly to Buchan in his capacity as a founder of the Football Writers' Association.

Meanwhile the last rites were twice read to Matt Busby in the Munich hospital where he spent 71 days fighting for his life.

In Busby's absence it was left to his loyal colleague, Jimmy Murphy – who had missed the Belgrade trip while managing the Welsh national team – to pick up the pieces.

Normally Murphy remained firmly on the sidelines. But in those vital few months after the crash he bore the brunt of the inevitable media frenzy. Without his leadership at this critical time it is more than likely that United would have crumbled.

Busby himself reckoned that it would take five years at least for the club to recover, and yet with a hastily assembled squad of veterans and raw youngsters, United somehow managed to reach the FA Cup Final, just three months after the disaster. They lost 2-0 to Bolton, but with four of the Munich survivors in the team (Harry Gregg, Bill Foulkes, Bobby Charlton and Dennis Viollet), won universal admiration for their pluck.

Even so, the next few seasons proved mightily difficult, as doubts arose as to whether Busby, now fully recovered, would be able to rebuild his team yet again. Of the other Munich survivors, Johnny Berry and Jackie Blanchflower would never play again, while Ken Morgans never recaptured his place in the first team. Meanwhile, despite the club's much vaunted youth system, the pressure now placed on some of the younger players became almost unbearable.

As the team faltered, so too did crowds drop at Old Trafford. Having topped the attendance charts from 1956–59, with averages ranging between 45–53,000, by 1961–62 they had fallen to less than 34,000, their lowest level since 1938–39.

Yet amid the gloom and lingering sense of loss, there were some rays of hope. Albert Scanlon, who had suffered a fractured skull at Munich, enjoyed a successful run, as did *Football Monthly* cover boy Wilf McGuinness (see above). Dennis Viollet set a record of 32 League goals in a season in 1959-60, and best of all, Bobby Charlton emerged as a cornerstone of the team.

Raised in the back streets of Ashington, Charlton had made his United debut in October 1956, and was only 20 at the time of Munich.

Nevertheless, for the first time in his managerial career Matt Busby was obliged to spend heavily in the transfer market. In came Sheffield Wednesday's Albert Quixall (whose tight shorts, see page 48, had provoked many a comment in *Football Monthly*), Noel Cantwell, Maurice Setters, David Herd, Pat Crerand and Denis Law – a record £115,000 signing from Torino in July 1962 – whilst players such as Nobby Stiles and Johnny Giles rose up from United's youth team.

But although victory came in the FA Cup in 1963 – Busby's fourth Wembley final – United struggled to

avoid relegation that same season, finishing in their lowest League position since 1937.

That, however, proved to be a rare blip. From the following season onwards, a new and supremely gifted United emerged, characterised by its three leading lights: Charlton, already a veteran in his mid 20s, the deadly predator Denis Law, and a starlet from Belfast, George Best, who made his debut in September 1963, aged 17. In time, all three would be voted European Footballer of the Year, a record for one club matched then only by Real Madrid. Charlton and Best were also made Footballers of the Year by the English Football Writers' Association.

United now regained their previous mantle, that of the country's most attractive outfit. At away grounds crowds packed to see Busby's third great team.

In line with this image, Old Trafford started to assume a modern appearance too, with its sleek new cantilevered stand, complete with football's first executive boxes, rising up on the north side in readiness for the following year's World Cup.

In season 1964–65 United's average gates of over 46,500 were the highest in the League.

But as articles in *Football Monthly* suggest, there were other, less savoury trends to note.

Denis Law, for example, who bagged a phenomenal 46 goals in 42 games during 1963-64, became notorious for his volatile temper; this at a time when referees clamped down far less on brutal defending than is the norm today.

To several commentators, Law exemplified all that was going wrong with football. On the field players' discipline appeared to be breaking down inexorably. On the terraces obscene chanting was becoming common. Hooliganism and pitch invasions were also starting to blight ▶

the game's reputation. (United would be one of the first clubs to install perimeter fences.)

The players' images changed also, partly owing to their greater access to the press, but mostly because the abolition of the maximum wage in 1961 allowed a much higher standard of living than most working men of a similar age, and even players only a few years their senior. In consequence, up and coming stars such as David Sadler, able to afford their own cars and large houses in the leafy suburbs, became increasingly disconnected from the fans who paid their wages.

George Best, famously, went further by becoming football's first modern celebrity, lauded as much for what he did off the field as on it. A marketing man's dream, Best was the first player to attract as many female fans as male ones.

Top footballers had long endorsed such products as football boots, Bovril and Brylcreem. But as well as representing Stylo Matchmakers (see page 94), Best became a model for the Manchester-based mail order giant, Great Universal Stores. He also lent his name to brands of sunglasses and aftershave. And while Charles Buchan had once run a sports outfitters – a business taken up by many a former pro – Best co-owned a chain of fashion boutiques.

Beatles-style, he even had his own fan club.

Not surprisingly, Best featured more on the pages of *Football Monthly* than any other player, with only one exception.

Denis Law's picture count in the magazine was the highest of all.

That might have been pure chance. Or was it perhaps recognition by the editors that amongst most fans the feisty Law was the player they most admired?

Throughout this stellar period, as regular tributes in *Football Monthly*

confirmed, Matt Busby remained the single most important individual at Old Trafford. Now held as an elder statesman, he reached his apotheosis by steering United to that long awaited European Cup victory on a glorious and emotional evening in May 1968.

Staged at Wembley, ten years after Munich and broadcast live on black and white television, United's 4-1 win over Benfica captured the nation's attention.

Manchester City and Liverpool fans might have disagreed, but as *Football Monthly* editor Pat Collins wrote, United now enjoyed a 'unique position as the adopted national side'.

Without question the spectre of Munich played a part in this.

That night in 1968, many tears of joy and of sadness were openly shed by the crash survivors Matt Busby, Bobby Charlton and Bill Foulkes. But the same was also true of thousands of older supporters around Britain, remembering how close the Babes had been to a similar triumph in 1958.

Knighted soon after the 1968 final, Sir Matt had only one further season as manager before standing down at the age of 60. In his final season United again seemed en route to further European Cup honours, reaching the semi-finals. But they also finished only 11th in the table, and to many observers a fresh approach was clearly needed.

Yet how to succeed a man of such stature as Matt Busby?

The candidate chosen for this unenviable task, on Busby's recommendation, was an Old Trafford insider, Wilf McGuinness.

Manchester-born McGuinness had signed for United as a 16 year old in 1953, and made over 80 appearances as a wing half, winning two caps for England, before his career was cut short by a broken leg sustained in a reserve match

in December 1959 (ten months after he had appeared on the cover of *Football Monthly*, see previous page). But although he had since risen up the coaching ladder at Old Trafford, he was an unlikely choice to succeed Busby. Above all, at only 31 he was of the same generation as many of the first team.

These were turbulent times for United. Busby stayed on at the club in the newly created position of General Manager, leading to obvious speculation as to how much control McGuinness really wielded. For his part, Busby showed too much loyalty to some of the older players. The first of these to retire was Bill Foulkes, replaced by Arsenal's Ian Ure. But Charlton, Law and Best played on, the latter showing increasing signs of indiscipline.

As results deteriorated, matters reached a head in December 1970. McGuinness was humiliatingly demoted to reserve team coach, while Busby reluctantly stepped back into the breach until a replacement could be found. (McGuinness subsequently left Old Trafford a year later, apparently so traumatised that his hair fell out.)

His replacement, appointed in June 1971 and again heartily endorsed by Busby, was Irishman Frank O'Farrell. A former West Ham midfielder, O'Farrell had done well as manager at Weymouth, Torquay and Leicester City, and for his first few months at Old Trafford, despite a pre-season defeat by Halifax in the Watney Cup, and having to play two home games at neutral grounds as a punishment for crowd trouble, all seemed well. By Christmas 1971 United were top of the table.

But despite the arrival of big money signings Martin Buchan and Ian Storey-Moore, O'Farrell could not sustain the run and the team ended in eighth place.

Worse would follow the next season as two further expensive

signings, Ted MacDougall and Wyn Davies failed to make an impact.

With George Best now regularly failing to turn up for training and O'Farrell feeling undermined by both his chairman and by Sir Matt, United slipped further into crisis.

In December 1972 O'Farrell was replaced by the outspoken Scot, Tommy Docherty (who had cut his managerial teeth at Chelsea, Rotherham and Aston Villa).

Docherty saved United from relegation that season, but worse was to follow.

In April 1973 Bobby Charlton, the last of the Babes, played his final game for United. Denis Law left for Manchester City. David Sadler moved to Preston. A few months later, Ian Storey-Moore was forced to retire at the age of 28.

Meanwhile, in the London offices of *Football Monthly* another era was coming to an end. Unable to compete with the brasher new weeklies, in August 1973 the magazine announced its rebranding as a pocket-sized digest.

So it is, again by chance, that our selection from the Charles Buchan archive ends in the very season that saw United suffer their greatest humiliation since 1937 – relegation to the Second Division, just six years after being crowned as European Champions.

The wheel had come full circle.

Not until nearly two decades later would the legacy of the Busby era be laid permanently to rest when another great Scot, Alex Ferguson, finally restored United to the pinnacle of European football.

Life at modern day Old Trafford is a far cry from the days of *Charles Buchan's Football Monthly*.

But if the period 1951-73 tells us anything it is that in the world of football, and particularly in the world of Manchester United, nothing can ever, nor should ever be taken for granted.

All the excitement of our national game is captured in this glimpse of a Manchester United fan—snapped when United went to London for their gallant Cup battle at Wembley.

HURRAH—It's kick-off time again!

▲ September 1958

"Yes, I would do it all over again!"

by Matt Busby

AT the start of the 1928-29 soccer season, an eighteen-year-old boy came down to Manchester from Scotland bent on making soccer his career. I was that boy.

Now I am still in Manchester, no longer a player, of course, but manager of a successful club. And if you were to ask me if I had to start my career again would it be devoted to football, I should give a firm "Yes."

Soccer keeps both body and mind fit. No millionaire can use his money to aspire to the physical peak of bodily fitness which every footballer must reach.

You see, I have always been able to look upon myself as being fit as the proverbial fiddle. Soccer keeps you that way. That is why, if I had my career to start all over again, I should choose football as my means of livelihood.

It's a great life. It has its misfortunes, of course, but the young soccer player today has everything in his favour.

When Manchester City signed me on at £5 per week—a very good wage in those days, far in advance of anything an eighteen-year-old could earn in a sedentary occupation—I dreamed of the day when I should be able to justify my trip south.

The first objective was the senior League team with its automatic increase in wages. If I could achieve this ambition, I should be entitled to the maximum £8 per week.

That £8 was not subject to the tax we are compelled to face today. It was, most people contend, better money than the £12, to be increased to £14 in the present season, that players receive as a maximum now.

A benefit of £650 (I had one) in pre-war days was another great inducement, worth, perhaps, more than the £750 maximum benefit today. But, as I have said, it was the healthy life of soccer that appealed to me and it would be the same if I were eighteen years old again and meditating on my future in this commercial world of ours.

As a boy, I was football mad. I still am. I wanted to mould my life on something I really liked and loved. Football was the outlet. Fresh air and physical fitness make for good health which is worth more than a financial fortune.

I am not going to say I planned my life in soccer down to every detail. For example, I moved from Manchester City to Liverpool purely for domestic reasons that could not be foreseen.

Then came the war and I could not have taken that into consideration. But I had some thrilling experiences as physical training instructor on troopships.

Note the accent on physical fitness. The miles I ran round the decks of those ships before the troops were awake—because I realised, as I have always realised, that soccer and physical fitness must be in harmony.

The war ended and then, as I had planned during those six years, I found myself in a manager's job, the very one I wanted.

Before the war, there were few outlets for soccer players when their careers ended. Oh, yes, there was the possibility of a job as licensee of an hotel, but there were not sufficient hotels for all ex-players. In any event, that was not my plan. I had started in football determined that I should stay in it.

Football now offers richer inducements, I think, than in my early days. The young player of today, who makes a success of it, can be a contented fellow when the time comes for him to retire in, say, twelve or fifteen years. If he does not want to stay in the game, he should have enough money to his credit to start a business on his own or take up some other employment.

Look at the prospects. The player can participate in the Football Association vocational training scheme. He can

JENKINS by Nelward

MASSAGE ROOM

▲ October 1951

learn a trade or profession. The wonder to me is why some young players do not take full advantage of this scheme.

I know that, had we been given similar opportunities in my early playing days, it would have been a blessing to many old stars who have since fallen on hard times.

There is also the Provident Scheme for players by which they have ten per cent of their annual earnings placed in trust for the future.

This is not a deduction from their pay. It is an extra ten per cent added and put aside until the player reaches thirty-five years of age, or retires from the game.

Supposing a player has a £750 benefit one season. He gets a £75 grant (ten per cent) placed to his credit—and don't forget that this is free of tax. We never had such inducements dangled before *our* eyes.

Everything Provided

SOCCER, indeed, has improved in every way you look at it. There are coaches to teach the youngsters to become stars; players have the best medical attention and every facility for getting fit, and keeping fit, is available.

A kick on the ankle no longer means a long lay-off. The best electrical equipment and masseurs are there to get them physically fit after injury or illness.

It has always been a strong contention of mine—which I have advocated freely—that the players should receive the best wages and the best treatment. Now I think there is one minor item the legislators should tackle.

This concerns the player who is injured. He is compelled to remain idle, say, for a fortnight. Through no fault of his own, he cannot draw any bonus money that his team might earn during the period he is incapacitated.

The League allows only twelve players—the actual team and a reserve—to draw this bonus. I feel the injured man should be allowed to draw it just as he would have done if he had been fit and taking part in the game.

When he recovers, then he starts again from scratch. That is, he would not draw any bonus until he recaptured his place in the team and helped to earn it.

Though this is a minor detail, I hope the powers-that-be will give it serious consideration. There is nothing unfair in the suggestion and it would make the players feel more content. After all, I can see no reason why, if injured in the course of his work, a footballer should also suffer financially.

So I sum up: soccer is a great game, the greatest ambassador in the world. I would not change places with anybody.

To the young footballer who may be "wavering" I can only say that, if the ability is there, there is no need to hesitate. The game is attracting the manual worker as well as the cultured youth. There is room for both—and there are so many advantages to be gained, physical and financial.

ON THE MARK . . .

Year in, year out, there are few teams as consistent as Manchester United. Their record of four times runners-up in the League and a Cup Final victory in the last five years tells its own tale.

Here are the team: back row: T. Curry (trainer), J. Carey, W. Redman, A. Chilton, R. Allen, W. McGlen, J. Aston; front row: H. Cockburn, J. Downie, J. Rowley, S. Pearson, H. McShane.

Yes Sir!
BRYLCREEM
YOUR HAIR
for the CLEAN* smart look

Brylcreem is different—you can tell that at once. Different because its pure oils are emulsified to prevent excessive oiliness; because it's not greasy, not messy. Different because Brylcreem grooms your hair the healthy way, gives that *clean* smart look which goes hand in hand with success. Brylcreem *your* hair and see the difference. Brylcreem comes in tubs 1/6, 2/3 and 4/1, or handy tubes 2/3.

NOT GREASY ✓
NOT MESSY ✓

BRYLCREEM – THE PERFECT HAIRDRESSING

royds 137/116

Great names linked in sport

UMBRO
The Sportswear people

...AND OLD TRAFFORD

Old Trafford—the home of Manchester United—was badly blitzed during the war. It is quite close to Lancashire's famous Old Trafford cricket ground.

The best teams wear the best kit. "Umbro" pleases the best because the quality is superlative.

The choice of champions

OF LEADING SPORTS OUTFITTERS ALL OVER THE WORLD

A "Real" Man's Watch and a "Good" Boy's too

POCKET MODELS FROM **23'9**
5-JEWEL WRIST MODELS FROM **55'-**
WITH UNCONDITIONAL SIX MONTHS GUARANTEE.
Sold by Jewellers everywhere.

Y.201. Gilt Arabic figures. Chrome stainless steel case. £2 . 15 . 0

STANLEY MATTHEWS
Famous Blackpool and England Outside-right and Stanley Junior **BOTH VOUCH FOR THE DEPENDABILITY OF THEIR**

SMITHS
Empire
WATCHES

SMITHS ENGLISH CLOCKS LTD., SECTRIC HOUSE, LONDON, N.W.2.
The Clock & Watch Division of S. Smith & Sons (England) Ltd.

JOHNNY CAREY

whom supporters of Manchester United and Ireland will always remember with pride

JACK ROWLEY
Manchester United
and England

MANCHESTER UNITED

After a game with the town team I used to rush to see our League side play . . . now

I am in the place of my boyhood hero

STAN PEARSON . . . my hero who never seemed to play a bad game.

THE evening of April 30, 1954, was Cup Final Eve, only a few hours before the Wembley game between West Bromwich and Preston North End. It was on that evening, with Soccer fervour rising to a high pitch for the big game, that I played in my first major representative game.

Old England versus Young England was the tag given to this tussle at Highbury Stadium. Both teams had much incentive to win—the experienced players to prove they were still the best in the game; we youngsters to try and move further up the ladder of fame.

My team lost 2—1, but never have I felt it less a disgrace to be on the losing side.

As an inside-forward, I naturally had particular interest in the players occupying similar positions for Old England—Wilf Mannion and Len Shackleton.

What a display those two gave! Their wonderful tricks, skill, and defence-splitting passes brought home to me just how much I had to learn.

Their exhibition was something I had never seen before, and have not seen since. Absolute masters of their profession, they gave our defence a real gruelling, and taught me more than I have learned from any other dozen matches.

by DENIS VIOLLET
Manchester United

To top off a wonderful week-end, I had a stand seat for the Final the next day. But perhaps I expected too much, after watching Wilf and Len, for this game left me very disappointed.

If ever I felt sympathy for a player it was for Preston's Tommy Docherty, who had a penalty given against him from which West Bromwich scored.

Tommy had previously rallied his team magnificently. I would sooner play in front of this great Scot than against him, for he fights to the last second and refuses to admit defeat.

But there are many fine wing-halves in addition to Docherty.

For instance . . . Danny Blanchflower, Len Phillips, Jimmy Scoular, Bill Slater, Bill McGarry, Roy Paul. The list could go on for ever!

No other position seems to have such an abundance of stars. Even Billy Wright and Harry Johnston played on the wing before they switched to centre.

As a lad, my ambition was always to play for Manchester United. On Saturday mornings I would play for my local team, then rush off to watch the League side.

★

Stan Pearson, a dark-haired inside-left who never seemed to play a bad game, was my hero.

I little thought the day would come when I would be the player to succeed him in the United team.

But it happened—late in 1953, when the club struck a poor run and struggled near the bottom of the First Division.

Mr. Busby also brought in a number of other young players, like Duncan Edwards and Jackie Blanchflower. We had a no-score draw at Huddersfield, and seemed to blend together.

I do not feel enough credit was given to our captain and centre-half, Allenby Chilton, for the change in the team's fortunes.

With so many immature, inexperienced players round him, Chilton had to put

in tremendous work. He was a constant inspiration to us, and held the team together.

Tall and strong, he dominated the defence, quickly covered up mistakes, encouraged each player, and somehow found time occasionally to make a break-away on his own.

On the field, Chilton, who is now with Grimsby, never minced words. He would tell us exactly what was wanted—but never held off-field inquests.

Our manager, Mr. Busby, also has the art of criticising in such a way that you can always take his words without ill-feeling.

He has done much to improve my play, and we all realise that whatever he says is for our benefit and that of the team.

I well recall how, when I was fifteen and had decided to go to Old Trafford, I told former England goalkeeper Frank Swift of my choice.

"You will not find a better man anywhere than Matt Busby," Frank said. **"You should have a great future under him."**

I can give no better illustration of how players are considered at United than to mention the benefit payments recently made to four of us.

Each of us is a young player, none with five years' professional service. But we received maximum benefits—one year of amateur service counting in some cases.

Every player can recall his first League goal, and I am no exception—mainly because surprise nearly made me miss it.

We were playing West Bromwich, at Old Trafford. I got the ball, beat two men, and looked up. Bang in front of me was the goal.

For a moment I could not move my legs. Then I tried a shot. I miskicked the ball, but, luckily, it went into a corner of the net.

JACKIE BLANCHFLOWER . . . one of the youngsters Mr. Busby brought into the team.

▲ June 1955

Charles Buchan's
FOOTBALL
MONTHLY

1'6

Overseas Price 2/-
Forces Overseas 1/6

FEBRUARY, 1955

NIGHTMARE MATCH

by

RAY WOOD

Manchester United

and

England

MY NIGHTMARE MATCH

by RAY WOOD

Manchester United and England

★

Ray Wood saves from Bentley of Chelsea.

AS a youngster I always watched at least one Newcastle United game every season. That was when Manchester City were visitors. Early at the ground, I would rush in as soon as the gates were opened and grab the best place on the terraces.

There I waited anxiously for the teams to run out—and for one player in particular, the big City goalkeeper, green-sweatered Frank Swift.

This dark-haired king-pin keeper was my hero. His wonderful saves thrilled me as nothing else did. Wedged among the shouting crowd, I used to stare at him, wide-eyed, and wonder if I could ever be like him.

I have not, of course, reached anything like " Swifty's " standard, but I have been lucky enough to follow him into England's team.

My first game for England was in October, 1954, against Ireland, at Windsor Park, Belfast.

That day my dream of following " Swifty " came true—but I could hardly believe it. It seemed incredible.

For there have been times when I have despaired of making good. My path to a cap was not smooth, and never was I more disconsolate than on one Saturday afternoon in October, 1949. On the Friday evening I had just finished my tea, and was sitting back, thinking of Darlington's match the next day. I was playing.

Then a hurried message arrived from our manager Billy Forrest. He wanted to see me about a transfer.

" Transfer," I yelped. " Where to ? "

My father calmed me down and said he would come along. So off we went to the club. I was only eighteen.

Soon I knew the facts. A couple of days earlier, in a cup-tie against Crewe Alexandra, I had done well. Among the crowd was Manchester United's famous scout Louis Rocca.

He suggested that the First Division club should snap me up immediately, and, before I had time to gather my senses, I was shaking hands with manager Mr. Matt Busby.

Next morning I was in a car bound for Manchester and, a few hours later, turned

Continued

▲ February 1955

RAY WOOD
Continued

out against my former local club, Newcastle United, who had once signed me as an amateur.

A dream debut? It was not!

A nightmare is the only way I can describe the game.

Before I went on the field Mr. Busby told me not to worry, that I need not think I had to be any better because I was in a First Division team.

That sounded fine in the dressing room, but out on the pitch it was no consolation.

After twenty minutes, right-winger Tommy Walker put one past me, and although that was the only goal I let in—and we drew—I was a very unhappy youngster.

Despondent, I left the ground . . . to be cheered a little by my parents, but wondering, miserably, if I had not been too ambitious in switching to the First Division.

My confidence was shaken and it did not surprise me when I was dropped for the rest of the season.

But I *did* learn one vital lesson from that game—don't try to reach the top in one jump.

Another thing for which I'm thankful is that my father insisted I must finish my engineering apprenticeship. Football can be a precarious living. It's so easy to get a bad knock and find your livelihood swept away.

I have the consolation that if such a thing happens I can earn a living elsewhere.

When I was 15, Newcastle signed me

and I stayed with them for a spell, playing about 25 matches. But, with Jack Fairbrother, Eric Garbutt, and Jerry Lowery ahead in the queue there was obviously little hope of promotion.

Gateshead were keen to sign me, and so were Sunderland. I went to Roker Park but did not fancy the idea of a three-month trial so joined Darlington.

I got quick promotion at Darlington, I signed on a Wednesday and, three days later, deputised for injured Billy Dunn, who lived only 200 yards from my home.

That was the start of a three-month spell which ended with the transfer.

After the terrible start with Manchester United I dropped from the limelight. They had Jack Crompton as their No. 1

" Excuse me, are we playing home, away or draw on Saturday ? "

man, then Reg Allen joined at a fee reputed to be a record for a goalkeeper.

I began to wonder if a chance would come my way again. I got only an occasional senior appearance until Christmas Day, 1952, when I started a run which went into February.

Luck was against me, however, for I broke a wrist, the dread of all 'keepers. For the remainder of the season I was out.

Then came the day when I had to see if the weakness had really mended, by stopping a piledriver. I put my hand up to the ball, felt no pain, and could have jumped for joy.

So to my first big representative selection, against Italy's " Under 23," an honour which I got while in the Air Force.

Shortly after that I was chosen for England " B " against Scotland " B." I well remember how dangerous Portsmouth's Jackie Henderson was on the ice-covered Sunderland pitch.

Four days after that game I fell ill and did not kick a ball for the rest of the season.

I had been hurt in a friendly game some weeks earlier, but had played in the representative matches and League tussles not knowing I had an injured kidney.

So to this season . . . and what a season it has been !

Before I pulled on United's sweater again I had packed away my Air Force blue and been demobbed. But that was only the start of an astonishing spell.

Demobbed in July I had won both Football League and England honours within three months. I'm mighty proud of these awards and as I'm only 23 hope more will come my way.

DUNCAN EDWARDS
Manchester United

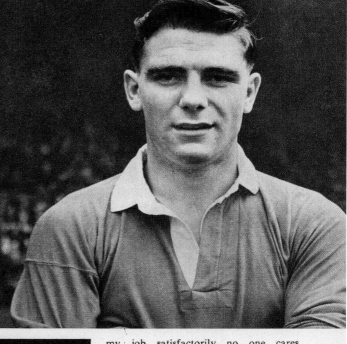

Nine months after quitting the class-room I made my Football League debut. When I went into the dressing room . . .

I thought I was back at school!

ALL footballers have one ambition—to play at the wonder Wembley Stadium. That lovely turf, huge crowds, in fact, the entire surroundings, put a match into a setting unequalled elsewhere.

I played there twice before I was FIFTEEN. Yet one Wembley trip is something many Soccer players never accomplish in a lifetime.

Nine schoolboy caps gave me a taste of top-line Soccer, for we played before big crowds and on the best grounds in the country.

After that, the thought of making my Football League debut was not terrifying. It was still a thrill, however, for it came only nine months after I had packed away my school books for the last time.

On leaving school I did not face the difficulty of most youngsters—finding a job. Football was my future; I had no lack of prospective employers.

Schoolboy internationals are always noted by the League clubs. I chose to go to Manchester United.

I thought my future would be better away from the Midlands, where I lived. And United had a great reputation for giving plenty of opportunities to young players and treating them in the best possible manner.

As a matter of fact, the first time I entered the dressing room to meet the other players I wondered if I was in the right place.

There were so many other youngsters that it seemed almost like being back at school. I found it very easy to settle down and make friends.

To return to my League debut. It came in the remarkable 1953 season when I won a medal with the club's successful under-18 team, and also turned out with the seniors.

I went to the ground one Friday morning and was called to manager Matt Busby's office. He quietly told me I was selected for the first team.

by DUNCAN EDWARDS
Manchester United and England

All I could think about was letting my mother and father know the news.

Four other teenage players had made a debut with United that season. Before me, outside-right John Scott, centre-forward Eddie Lewis, inside-forward John Doherty and left-winger David Pegg, had all been selected.

It showed just what opportunity there was for a youngster at Old Trafford.

I had only that one league outing during the season (we lost 4—1 to Cardiff City) but mid-way through the next season I had won a permanent place.

I would like to pay tribute to one of the biggest little players I have met. He is international wing-half Henry Cockburn, whose place I eventually took.

For quite a spell Henry was on the injured list. He watched our home games and before the kick-off he would come into the dressing room and give me tips about my opponent. Those tips usually proved invaluable to me.

There are stories told of experienced players getting jealous of a youngster succeeding them. I have never come across this, nor found older players trying to intimidate me.

Whatever teams I have played with —club, F.A. under 23, Football League or England —I have been accepted on level terms by my colleagues. My youth has meant nothing.

So long as I do my job satisfactorily no one cares whether I am 17 or 70.

The first trip I had abroad was with the under-23 team to Bologna, to meet the Italians. They put it over us and were a very much faster, better-thinking side **on the day.**

I stress, on the day, because there always comes another day. We got to grips again—almost 12 months later—and came out of the tussle with a smashing win, at Stamford Bridge, Chelsea.

They had a much changed attack but Guiseppe Virgilli, known as "Golden Boy" in Italy, and rated in the £40,000 class, led their attack again.

He got little change from Birmingham's Trevor Smith who, with Ron Flowers and I, formed a half-back line with an average age of 19.

England's team-building plans certainly give young players a first-class chance to know each other before winning promotion to the international side.

Also, friendship built on and off the field seems to lead to better combination.

I think the most exciting game I can recall from my brief spell as a League player came in May, 1954. It happened on Cup Final Eve.

Floodlit matches always seem to have an extra bit of glamour, and this time I was a member of the Young England side against Old England at Highbury.

The opposing forward line certainly gave us the run around that evening. Matthews, Mannion, Lawton, Shackleton and Langton—I'll always remember that line-up.

They set out to play exhibition football, while beating us—and managed to do both. This was one occasion on which it was no disgrace to be beaten.

Another veteran I always admire and enjoy playing against is Sheffield United's Jimmy Hagan, who has fine ball skill.

I must not give the impression that I think all the best inside-forwards are the older ones. As good as any is Albert Quixall, who never gets sufficient credit for the amount of hard work and chasing he does.

It's wonderful to be among them all, getting paid for what I most enjoy doing.

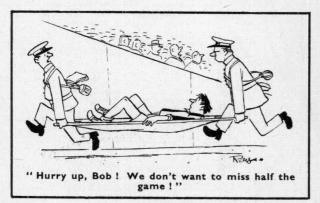

"Hurry up, Bob! We don't want to miss half the game!"

Behind the scenes at Manchester United

Far away from the roaring crowd manager Matt Busby enjoys a spot of putting with his wife.

Mr. Busby, former Scottish international star, passes on a few tips from his rich experience to United's youngsters.

▲ 1955–56 Gift Book

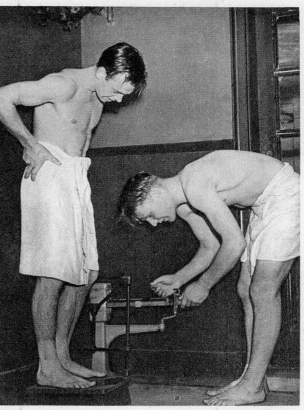

A fine study of trainer Tom Curry and assistant-trainer Bill Inglis.

Colin Webster keeps an eye on his weight as Mark Jones adjusts the scales.

Canasta relaxes David Pegg, Colin Webster and Tommy Taylor.

MANCHESTER UNITED

Standing—Whitefoot, Foulkes, Wood, Jones, Blanchflower, McGuinness.
Sitting—Berry, Webster, Byrne, Taylor, Pegg.

▲ February 1956

SOCCER EXPERTS SAY—

extra energy makes the difference!

DUNCAN EDWARDS

Manchester United's great discovery and, at 18, the youngest player for fifty years to win a full cap for England, says:

"Playing in top gear until the final whistle can really take it out of you. That's why I find 'Dextrosol' Glucose Tablets so handy. They're a natural source of energy you can rely on, anytime, anywhere."

Dextrosol

gives extra energy

To produce energy, your body burns fuel. A doctor will tell you that glucose is the fuel manufactured by your body from the food you eat. 'Dextrosol' is pure glucose: the quick, *natural* source of energy. 'Dextrosol' requires no digestion but passes straight into your bloodstream, carrying energy at once to muscles, nerves and brain.

To build up energy for that extra effort, to replace energy after exertion, eat delicious 'Dextrosol' Glucose Tablets. The handy packets slip easily into your pocket. 'Dextrosol' is the natural way of renewing energy—it can do you nothing but good, and there's no limit to the amount you can eat.

For extra energy—whenever you need it!

Look for the handy red and green packets, 10½d and 6d. Buy a packet today— **'Dextrosol' Glucose Tablets are now available at chemists and grocers everywhere!**

DEXTROSOL glucose tablets
BRAND

MADE BY THE PHARMACEUTICAL DIVISION OF BROWN & POLSON LTD.

▲ January 1957

The day I scored against my

FIVE years as reserve to a star can be an awful long time. You begin to wonder whether the man who is keeping you out of the first team will ever falter. Will your chance ever come? That's the question which passes through your thoughts a thousand times.

That was my position at Manchester United. Steady and apparently unshakeable in the first team was centre-half Allenby Chilton.

In three seasons I got a diminishing number of games. In 1950/51 I was chosen four times for the seniors. Next season I got three games . . . then two . . . and none at all in 1953/4.

About this time a bit of cross-talk started which became a standard joke in the dressing-room. Each morning on arrival I would go over to Allen and ask him: "How do you feel today?"

Bright and breezy he would reply: "Champion, just champion. I can go on for two or three years yet."

And until 1955 it seemed he would. Fortunately, I was at a great club, to me the best in the game, otherwise I probably might not have remained content. But I knew that when a chance came

manager Matt Busby would see I got it.

March 10, 1955, was the bright day of my career, for then I started a regular run. Chilton was rested and I came in against Cardiff City. Opposing me was Trevor Ford but I wasn't worried, having faced him when he was with Sunderland.

I had a fairly good game and after the match Allen came to congratulate me. It wasn't long before I was shaking his hand again and wishing him good luck as he went off to a new job as player-manager of Grimsby Town.

Ford didn't score in that game and, in fact, twelve successive leaders failed to

do so. Chelsea's Roy Bentley proved my unlucky thirteen and did the trick in the final game of the season.

Chelsea were champions by the time we played this game and little did I think that a year later we would have taken the trophy from them.

But 1955/6 was a wonderful season. I played in every League match, scored four goals and ended up with a First Division championship medal.

I think we were undoubtedly the youngest team, average age round 22, to win this competition. We were a happy crowd and I think this was reflected in

CHAMPIONSHIP CHEER
Tommy Taylor (left) and Roger Byrne celebrate after their win over Blackpool had given Manchester United the championship last season.

▲ January 1957

great goal—own side!

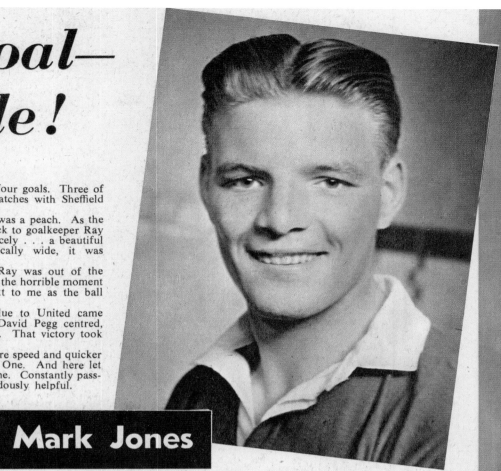

by Mark Jones

MANCHESTER UNITED CENTRE-HALF

the team's play. Now about those four goals. Three of them I put into my own net in matches with Sheffield United, Portsmouth and Charlton !

The one against Sheffield United was a peach. As the ball came to me I went to lob it back to goalkeeper Ray Wood. I did that part of the job nicely . . . a beautiful side-foot kick, arm flung majestically wide, it was certainly stylish.

Unfortunately I hadn't realised Ray was out of the goal. And perhaps you can imagine the horrible moment when I found he was standing next to me as the ball sailed into the net.

The one goal which was of value to United came against Birmingham. Left-winger David Pegg centred, I ran up and headed in the winner. That victory took us to the top of the Division.

I found better positional sense, more speed and quicker thinking were necessary in Division One. And here let me pay tribute to skipper Roger Byrne. Constantly passing advice and tips, he was tremendously helpful.

As a schoolboy, I got four England caps, being selected in different positions each time. Starting at left-back I was then chosen left-half, right-half and finally centre-half.

In the last of these games we met Ireland, at Old Trafford. A team-mate was Denis Viollet and a few years later we linked again in the United side.

After school, I had offers to join many clubs. Why did I pick United ? Well, they were famous. But, most of all, everyone spoke highly of their good treatment and I had never heard of players wanting to leave the club.

I think it was a little disappointing to my father that I set myself on the road to a football career. He thought I could make myself a nice future as a boxer.

After working my way through third and second teams I got my League début against Sheffield Wednesday on October 7, 1950, Allen Chilton having been selected for England.

Worried ? Not in the least. I've never been bothered about big crowds. I like the atmosphere and playing at home I naturally got encouragement from the crowd.

Johnny Carey and Johnny Aston were our full-backs then and they were a magnificent pair. Carey always had time to do his own work and yet look after me as well if I got into trouble.

One other great memory was going on United's trip to America. The trip on the *Queen Elizabeth* was a dream.

Every time we set out to play in a game a speed cop escort came with us blaring a passage with their sirens.

I celebrated my 19th birthday in America but Spurs spoilt it for me. We played them in an exhibition game and lost 7-1.

From that trip I still treasure photographs taken with Bob Hope and Bing Crosby.

"I hadn't realised Ray Wood was out of his goal until I had scored against him !" Here is Ray (left) on a happier occasion — with Byrne, holding the League trophy.

CHARLES BUCHAN'S FOOTBALL MONTHLY

Edited by—CHARLES BUCHAN
and JOHN THOMPSON
Associate Editor—J. M. SARL

APRIL, 1957 - - - No. 68

CONTENTS

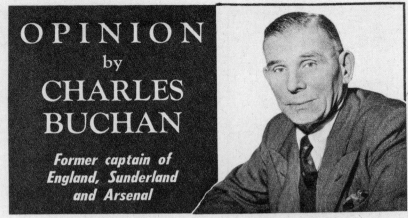

OPINION by CHARLES BUCHAN

Former captain of England, Sunderland and Arsenal

Russians must be in any European League

THE F.A. and the League Management Committee have taken the first steps towards the start of a European mid-week championship, to be played under flood-lights.

Invitations are being sent to officials in France, Spain, Belgium, Italy and the three home countries for an exploratory conference in London during April.

In view of the success of the European Cup in general, and Manchester United in particular, it is a wise step to take. But I do not expect any startling developments to come from it.

Eventually, a European Super-League, including the best team from every country in Europe, will materialise. **But not yet.**

In the meantime, any competition that will lead to better entertainment for the British public is welcome.

I understand the main idea at present is to link an English floodlight competi-tion with the present European Cup.

I feel, however, that no tournament will be qualified to bear the label " European " until countries behind the Iron Curtain, especially Russia, play a part in it.

Visits of Spartak and Dynamo aroused tremendous interest in this country. There is no doubt Russian teams can hold their own with any other European teams.

The appearances of Arsenal and Wolverhampton Wanderers in Moscow also brought happy results as far as the onlookers were concerned.

A competition without the Russians would not really be representative of Europe.

At the moment, however, a little pro-gress is better than none. A competition that brought teams like Real Madrid from Spain, and crack Italians to this country would, I am sure, attract huge mid-week attendances.

But we cannot take too big a step forward without weighing up the conse-quences.

Anything that would cut across our League organisation would, I feel, be disastrous.

There is, though, no reason why some English clubs should not join in immedi-ately.

Which clubs should represent England ? That is the big question.

Undoubtedly the fairest way would be for the clubs to fight it out among them-selves. To stage a tournament of which the winners would earn the rich prize of a place in the European Cup.

For example, the teams could be divided into say eight districts for the first stage. They would meet each other twice on a League basis and the winners go forward to a knock-out competition. The two to reach the final would be the lucky pair.

〜〜〜〜〜〜〜〜〜〜〜

Manchester United man-ager Matt Busby helps Jackie Blanchflower with a puzzle—the only type of crossword known at happy Old Trafford.

▲ April 1957

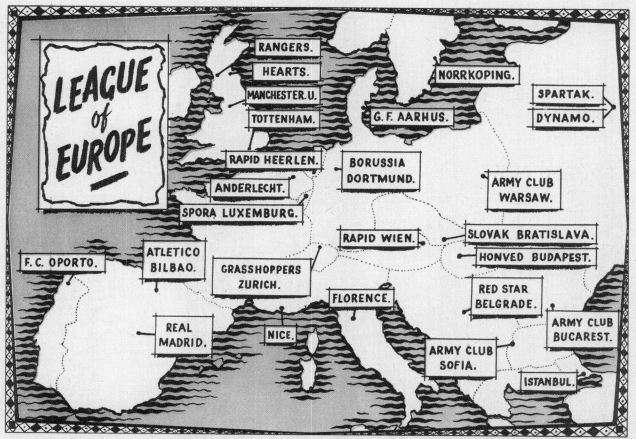

LEAGUE of EUROPE

RANGERS.
HEARTS.
MANCHESTER. U.
TOTTENHAM.
NORRKOPING.
SPARTAK.
DYNAMO.
G. F. AARHUS.
RAPID HEERLEN.
BORUSSIA DORTMUND.
ANDERLECHT.
ARMY CLUB WARSAW.
SPORA LUXEMBURG.
RAPID WIEN.
SLOVAK BRATISLAVA.
HONVED BUDAPEST.
F. C. OPORTO.
ATLETICO BILBAO.
GRASSHOPPERS ZURICH.
RED STAR BELGRADE.
FLORENCE.
REAL MADRID.
NICE.
ARMY CLUB SOFIA.
ARMY CLUB BUCAREST.
ISTANBUL.

A glimpse of things to come in the European League ! While our artist's map does not, of course, include all the possible entrants for a League of this type it does give an impression of the enormous scope which such a tournament would have.

Continued

Each team entering would thus be assured of several games. They would bring extra revenue and be a blessing to those now struggling to make ends meet.

Frankly, I do not think the mid-week games would have much effect on Saturday's League gates.

They would not bring back the millions that seem to have got out of the habit of attending Soccer games, but they would, at least, give the ardent fan something to cheer and talk about.

Manchester United's great achievements this season will always provide a topic for discussion. I cannot recall any finer performance than their defeat of Bilbao after giving the Spanish team a two goal start in the first leg.

Much of the credit for United's success goes to manager Matt Busby, the quietly-speaking Scot who played for his country and who still trains with his youngsters.

Busby has not made the common mistake of trying to make his team play to a set plan. He treats each game as a separate occasion, calling for different

~~~~~~~~~~~~

A bouquet for Manchester United skipper Roger Byrne from a Spanish senorita before the start of the second game with Bilbao.

treatment. That is Manchester United's secret.

On one occasion Matt told me:

" You can never judge what the opposition is likely to do. Any plans should be based on the skill and adaptability of your own players."

That was the reason for Arsenal's success during the 1930s. The players were not restricted in any way. They pooled their brains in the interests of the side.

And, like the Arsenal men, United's boys form part of a happy club. If they are dropped from the First Division side, they do not immediately ask for a

transfer. They work harder than ever to win back a place in the team.

There are some like Irish international Jackie Blanchflower and Wilf McGuinness, without a regular place, who are almost up to international standard.

They are content to wait for their chance, knowing it will come.

There can be no finer tribute to Matt Busby's shrewdness and tact, the discipline that prevails in United's ranks and the skill and harmony of the players than their record.

Since the war, United have won the League championship twice, been runners-up four times and once F.A. Cup winners.

Continued

Bilbao goalkeeper, Carmelo, clears a Manchester United raid during the European Cup game, which the Babes won by 3-0—and so brought glory to British football.

Continued

By the way, I hope United's players will be rewarded in some measure for the European Cup exploits.

I know the League rules prohibit payments above the maximum wage, but exceptions are made in the cases of bonus money and talent money for League and F.A. Cup games.

A player in a Cup-winning side receives £20 bonus and £50 talent money—that is if he has played in all previous rounds. I suggest a similar amount (£70) should be paid to United's players for each successful round in the European Cup.

United's victory over Bilbao, the Spanish champions, brought great prestige to British football.

Remember, United started the second leg of the European Cup-tie at Maine Road two goals down. They had been beaten 5-3 in Bilbao. Under the Maine Road, Manchester, floodlights, they gave an exhibition that would have graced a novel.

For 43 minutes, United's youngsters battled against tough, experienced opponents who, determined to hold on to their lead, waged a defensive battle. Then inside-right Dennis Viollet smashed the ball into the net.

In the second half, excitement swelled to a crescendo. Even when they had two goals disallowed for offside, United kept pegging away. In the 71st minute centre-forward Tommy Taylor scored with a wonderful left-foot shot. In the 85th minute outside-right John Berry made the score 3-0 and put Manchester United into the semi-final.

The scenes that followed were almost beyond description. The 65,000 onlookers gave United's players an ovation that has rarely been equalled anywhere.

Of 11 heroes, wing half-backs Duncan Edwards and Eddie Colman, and Taylor, were outstanding. But all played magnificent parts.

★

WHEN writing about the new Spanish tactics in the February edition of "Monthly," I stated that the new system, known in Spain as the "Spanish Bolt," was the combined work of the Soccer coaches of Catalonia.

I have received a letter from Mr. Manuel Fresco Maroto in which he points out that it is his work alone. I wish to give him credit for a well-planned scheme.

Mr. Maroto, a former Spanish star player and referee, works, I understand, entirely on his own. He has made a fine contribution to the game.

★

I WANT to pay tribute to the stirring deeds of Third Division South teams, Millwall and Bournemouth in our own F.A. Cup.

Millwall were knocked-out eventually by Birmingham but Bournemouth went on to surprise everyone by baffling Tottenham Hotspur into defeat at Dean Court.

At the time of writing I am waiting to hear how Bournemouth fared in the sixth round tie against Manchester United but whatever the outcome Bournemouth's triumphs of this season have assured them of a proud place in Soccer history.

Their earlier 1-0 defeat of Wolverhampton Wanderers at Molineux, was undoubtedly the best performance of the competition. It was accomplished by a team that cost less than £4,000.

Manager Freddie Cox, former Spurs and Arsenal player, who made a name for himself by winning Cup-ties with timely goals, is the man behind the Bournemouth scenes.

He has made his men team-conscious, with everyone pulling his full weight.

A team that can beat Wolves at their own fast, hard-tackling game deserves success.

★

IT is always good to hear of the whereabouts of League players who have left their clubs and found other jobs.

Many of you will remember Australian centre-half Joe Marston, who captained Preston North End twelve months ago.

Joe returned to his native Sydney last summer and was immediately made captain of the Leichhardt-Annandale team there. He led them to victory in the New South Wales State Cup final.

Another League player of whom I have heard is Bill Walsh, Sunderland and Darlington half-back. It does not seem very long since I saw him play for Darlington in a replayed F.A. Cup-tie at Walthamstow against the Avenue.

Walsh is now in Sydney, Australia, and captain of Sydney Hakoah. He was the key man in the Hakoah team which won the Southern Second Division championship and the Southern League knock-out Cup.

July 1957 ▶

BOBBY CHARLTON (Manchester United)

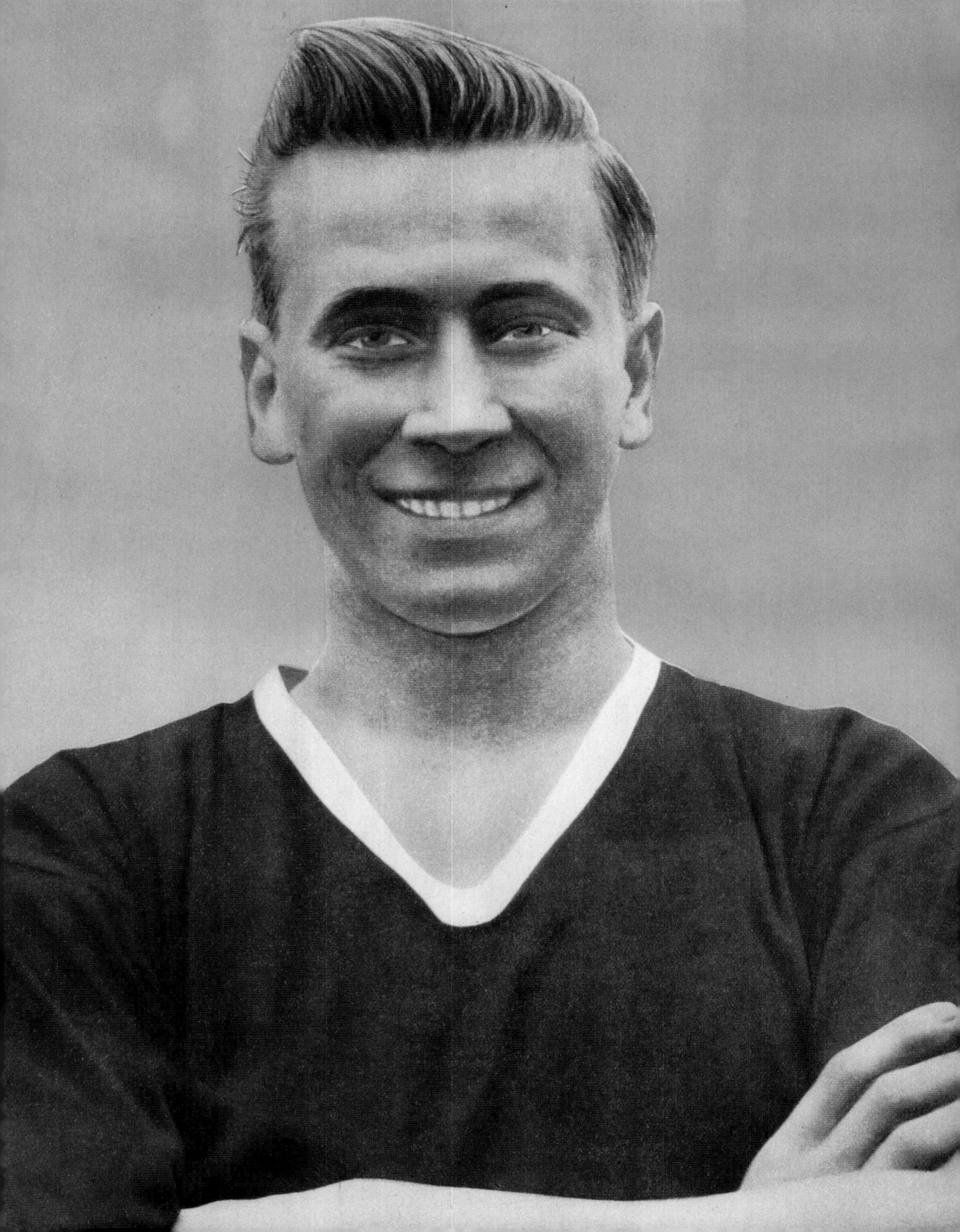

ROGER BYRNE
Manchester United and England

ROGER BYRNE
Star of the Season

AT the end of each season, "Football Monthly" selects a "Player of the Year." I have no hesitation, this time, in awarding the honour to Roger Byrne, Manchester United left-back.

Not only has he played in every England international, but he has led his side to victory in the League championship for the second year running, to the final of the F.A. Cup and to the semi-final of the European Cup.

Though the fame of John Charles, Wales and Leeds United centre-half transferred to Italian club Juventus, and the exploits of Tom Finney, Preston North End's centre-forward discovery, have commanded a lot of attention, there can be no denying the wonderful stimulus given by Byrne to both the England and Manchester United teams.

His cool, calculated work at left-back, either when his men are in winning mood or fighting to avoid defeat, have been an inspiration. He rarely plays a poor game.

Of course, Byrne has his detractors who assert that he is too inclined to take risks and prone to lose his balance at times.

But one of the reasons why Byrne is undoubtedly the best full-back in the country today is his confidence in his own ability. What appear to be risks—and would be risks to the ordinary player—are part and parcel of Byrne's immaculate style.

The square pass back from the bye-line to his goalkeeper and the bold dash forward to assist the attack come naturally to Byrne, who started his career as a forward and has complete command of the ball.

And if Byrne occasionally resents the attention paid to him or his colleagues, it is because he is so whole-heartedly immersed in the game. That he is the captain of United proves that these rare moments are insignificant.

Byrne is still comparatively young, 27 years of age. The longer he plays, the better he will become. He has the brains to make the best use of his great skill.

Born in Manchester, he has been a United man first and foremost. He has played a conspicuous part in their many successes.

Byrne is not only a quick thinker but very fast on the run. He has the speed to cope with the fastest of modern wing forwards. And the positional sense to limit their activities.

Most important of all, Byrne always uses the ball to advantage. His well-timed clearances have started many England and United attacks from within their own quarters.

With either foot, Byrne places the ball from his full-back position, straight to the feet of his forwards. It is a relic of his youthful days when he put across many accurate centres from outside-left.

Byrne is busy, too, planning for the future. He is training hard to qualify as a physiotherapist and I have no doubt he will become as skilled in this art as he is on the soccer field. C. B.

▲ August 1957

◀ 1957–58 Gift Book | ▲ November 1955 | February 1957

"AFTER HALF TIME, TED DALTON, THE MANCHESTER UNITED PHYSIOTHERAPIST, TOOK A BALL TO THE REAR OF THE STADIUM WHERE HE TESTED WOOD BY

throwing and kicking the ball to him, but poor Ray focused no more than a couple out of every six balls sent to him. It was a depressing session staged on that deserted grass strip outside the packed stadium, but a young Cockney kid who arrived to take a look at the performance did relieve the tension somewhat when he told Ray, ' Look Mister, my mates and me have got a game on just round the corner. You can come and play with us if you like.' Imagine the situation . . ."

Just one of the sidelights from the inside-soccer book all football fans have been waiting for

MATT BUSBY
My Story

220 pages, 50 photos 15/-.

Now, at last, the chief architect of Manchester United's fantastic success story tells of how it has been achieved and what it has meant to his own life. He tells of early struggles at the end of the war, faced with a bank overdraft and a blitzed ground . . . the inside stories of the big signings . . . the 1948 Cup Final against Blackpool described as the greatest ever . . . he spotlights the personalities of his leading players and then shares with the reader the biggest decision of his career when he painlessly tore apart a great side and banked his faith on youth.

European Cup 1956/7 . . . an artist called Di Stefano . . . Bilbao snowstorm trouble . . . tensest 90 minutes I have ever experienced . . . Bill Whelan's secret . . . Spanish officials demand photos . . . last minute snags could have put off both Real Madrid games . . . perfection in beating Anderlecht 10—0.

Spotlight on Carey, Chilton, Cockburn and the rest . . . building a great team . . . Tommy Taylor arrives from Barnsley . . . my big worry about Irishman Jackie Blanchflower . . . a trio of schoolboy stars, Duncan Edwards, David Pegg and Eddie Colman . . . how the United system works and what a boy must live up to.

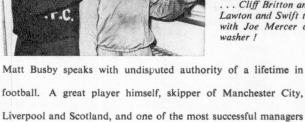

A pitman's cottage in Lanarkshire produces the original Busby Babe . . . signed by Manchester City . . . remarkable Cup Finals against Everton and Portsmouth . . . a boy called Frank Swift . . . happy days at Liverpool . . . wartime adventures . . . Cliff Britton and his Army lorry . . . Lawton and Swift take over the baggage with Joe Mercer chief cook and bottle washer !

Matt Busby speaks with undisputed authority of a lifetime in football. A great player himself, skipper of Manchester City, Liverpool and Scotland, and one of the most successful managers of all time, he does not shirk the controversial issues of the game.

In this book from his unique knowledge he discusses such matters as

- Problems of 1957 soccer in Britain
- The real reasons behind the John Charles and Tommy Taylor sensations
- The unfortunate business at Sunderland
- The truth of my £100,000 offer from Italy
- The question of substitutes
- Football abroad—how good are these foreigners?
- The Continental approach

BILL WHELAN
Manchester United
and
Republic of Ireland

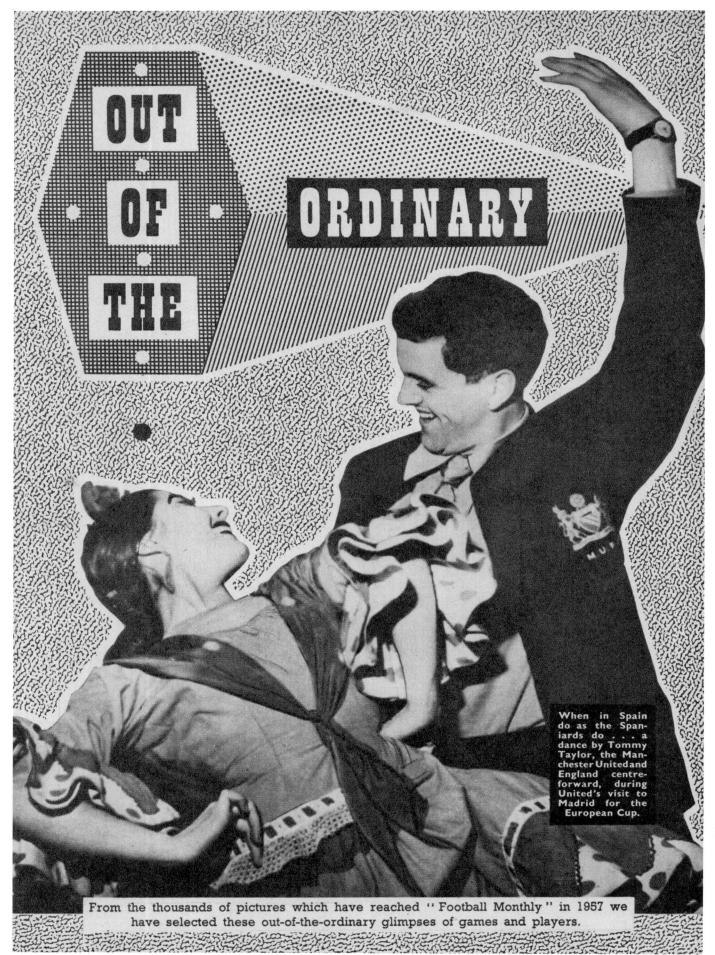

OUT OF THE ORDINARY

When in Spain do as the Spaniards do . . . a dance by Tommy Taylor, the Manchester United and England centre-forward, during United's visit to Madrid for the European Cup.

From the thousands of pictures which have reached "Football Monthly" in 1957 we have selected these out-of-the-ordinary glimpses of games and players.

▲ September 1957

Charles Buchan's
FOOTBALL
MONTHLY

DECEMBER 1957

1'6

Overseas Price 2/-
Forces Overseas 1/6

EDDIE COLMAN
Manchester United

ROGER BYRNE . . . captain and
left-back of the Mighty Busby Babes.

RAY WOOD . . . the
always brilliant goalkeeper,
makes a spectacular sky-
clutching leap.

Talent worth a fortune in transfer fees: Back row—Whitefoot, Colman, Foulkes,
Wood, Byrne, Blanchflower, Edwards. Front row—Berry, Whelan, Taylor,
Viollet, Pegg.

▲ January 1958

JACKIE BLANCHFLOWER ..
ited centre-half, sharpens up
with the aid of a punchball.

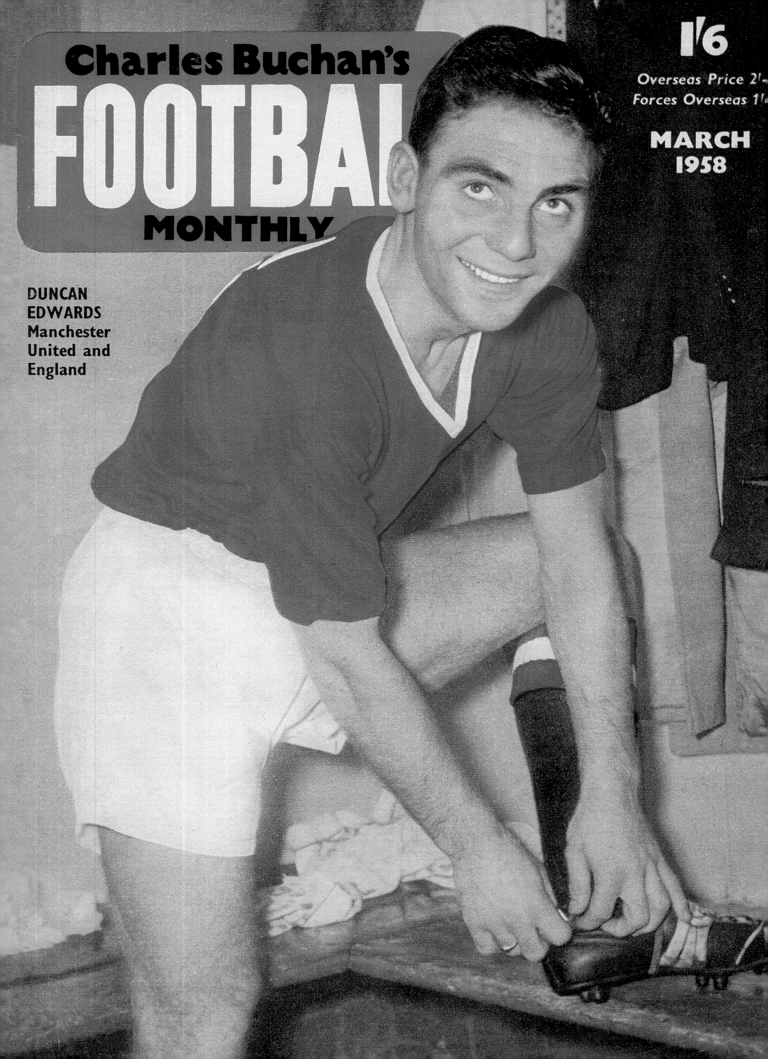

Charles Buchan's
FOOTBAL
MONTHLY

1'6
Overseas Price 2'-
Forces Overseas 1'

MARCH 1958

DUNCAN
EDWARDS
Manchester
United and
England

Every reader of "Football Monthly" will join with the staff of our magazine in expressing deepest sympathy to the relatives of the Manchester United men who died in the tragic air crash on their way home from Belgrade.

This edition was produced some days before the accident occurred. We hope that our front cover will be taken as a tribute and a reminder of happier days.

To our fine friends who died it can truly be said:

"In their death they were not divided: they were swifter than eagles, they were stronger than lions."

▲ late insertion to March 1958 (courtesy of the Manchester United Museum)

We will remember them . . .

BENT

COLMAN

JONES

WHELAN

TAYLOR   PEGG

ROGER BYRNE

DUNCAN EDWARDS

DESPITE the many thousands of words that have been written about the terrible air disaster on February 6 that cut down so many Manchester United players and officials, I find it difficult to realise they will no longer delight us with their skill and courage.

United had become world-famous, even to a greater extent than Arsenal in their palmy years. They owed a great deal to the sportsmanship, the ability and the team spirit of great men like Roger Byrne, Geoffrey Bent, Eddie Colman, Mark Jones, Bill Whelan, Tommy Taylor, David Pegg, and Duncan Edwards.

To the relatives of these lovable young men who lost their lives I extend, on behalf of many "Football Monthly" readers who have asked me to do so, and my staff, our deepest sympathy. May time heal the deep wounds inflicted.

And to those United members severely injured, like Matt Busby and Johnny Berry, I sincerely hope they will soon be restored to complete health; and that before long they will be able to take up life's threads where they were broken.

To me personally, it has been a great shock. I had seen them, at Highbury the previous Saturday, give a wonderful exhibition of Soccer, one of the best for many years. I thought then, United, blossoming further with more experience, would become the finest Soccer machine of the century.

Adding to the shock was the loss of so many journalistic friends with whom I had travelled to many corners of the earth and spent so many happy hours.

They were able men who wrote about the game and players without fear or favour.

Since the war, Manchester United have been without rival in League, F.A. Cup and European Cup.

It was a team of experts playing for the good of the side as a whole. And now some of those experts have passed away, their parts in the victory plan will not be overlooked or forgotten.

England, too, will sorely miss the artistry and wholehearted work of Byrne, Edwards and Taylor.

I have been in the company of these outstanding players many times. Their modest, unassuming behaviour was a credit to their club and to their country.

Every day that passes, I receive messages of sympathy from all over the world. I pass them on to United officials with a sad heart. With the memorial words of former heroes: *"At the going down of the sun and in the morning, we will remember them."*

CHARLES BUCHAN.

BILLY FOULKES
Manchester United
and England

THE BEGINNING OF MANCHESTER UNITED'S BRAVE FIGHT BACK

Shattered by the terrible air disaster in Munich in which so many fine players died, Manchester United began their gallant fight back to greatness by beating Sheffield Wednesday in the fifth round of the F.A. Cup. Our picture shows Billy Foulkes, the United captain, shaking hands with Wednesday's Albert Quixall.

▲ 1958–59 Gift Book

FREDDIE GOODWIN

Manchester United

says

(from experience)

you are on a sticky wicket if you try to play

CRICKET AND SOCCER
— *THEY DON'T MIX*

CAN a footballer afford to spend his summers playing first-class cricket? I have often asked myself that question since I have been at Old Trafford—a convenient centre for my dual career with Manchester United and Lancashire C.C.C. a couple of seasons or so ago.

In my case, the answer was 'No'. But before I could decide on which sport I was going to concentrate, Lancashire let me go.

Since then I have been able to settle down quite happily to my football.

I was not too happy about spending all the summer rest months playing three-day cricket. I know some Soccer players can do it.

But I was a fast bowler still in the process of building up strength—I am only 25 now—and I was convinced it would not work out.

Mind you, I enjoyed my cricket with Lancashire, and appeared in numerous championship games for them.

I was disappointed when they let me go after a couple of seasons, but I missed two or three highly attractive United tours abroad while I was playing cricket, and had no time for a summer holiday before reporting for Soccer training.

In July, 1955, I injured my back in a county game, had no real treatment until I saw a specialist, and started football training long after the other players.

Now, in a club like United, where competition is so keen, you can't afford to miss the pre-season practice games, otherwise you may not get the chance to earn a place in the side.

Now I'm in a position where I have a great chance to make a regular First Division spot my own. Admittedly, the tragic Munich disaster, which hit us so cruelly, has presented me with a great opportunity I may not otherwise have had, but I mean to make the most of it.

Of course, I'd played in United's League side before Munich. In fact, I made my first-team debut as far back as November, 1954, against Arsenal at Old Trafford. Albert Scanlon, our left-winger, came in for the first time that day.

I was at left-half, and played five games that season. Before that I'd had a job even to make the reserves, so well stocked were United with wing-halves.

Then Henry Cockburn was transferred to Bury and I got in at right-half in the Central League team. First-team regulars then were Geoff Whitefoot and Don Gibson.

" . . . It's fantastically exciting . . . Watch this ! "

At the start of the 1955-56 campaign, the League side suffered a couple of awkward injuries, and manager Matt Busby moved Duncan Edwards into attack. Again I had a few first-team outings.

Then a recurrence of my cricket injury put me out of the side, and young Eddie Coleman got his chance to take over.

I had little chance to shine again, although I did keep Eddie out for a short spell last season.

So Munich found me plodding along in the reserves, and I was glad to get the chance to help out when we were so sorely stricken.

We couldn't have wanted better support after that tragedy. I shall never forget the fantastic reception we got from the loyal Old Trafford crowd.

Like many of my colleagues at Old Trafford, I began my United career with the MUJACS after attending Chorlton County Secondary School. I was an inside-forward in those days—1949—but made little headway.

Then I went into the Army, served with the Royal Tank Regiment in Egypt in 1951, and got my first experience as a wing-half in army Soccer.

Two years later I returned to Old Trafford and, after a spell as an amateur, became a United professional —which I've never had cause to regret.

I still manage to keep my hand in at cricket. I've had a spell as professional with Ratcliffe, and play in local club games now and again. One doesn't lose one's love for cricket very easily.

▲ October 1958

Framed in a railway carriage window are four of the men who have made Manchester United respected and admired wherever football is played . . . Matt Busby, Harry Gregg, Billy Foulkes and Bobby Charlton.

THE MOST SUCCESSFUL FOOTBALL BOOT FOR MANY YEARS IS UNDOUBTEDLY

THE BOBBY CHARLTON MOULDED SOLE BOOT

For the 1960 Season it is further improved by being first in the field with **ALL WHITE** sole and studs. The sole with amazing properties.

Whilst retaining flexibility it eliminates lateral movement which twists ankles.

Mud-clinging is vastly reduced and of course it is guaranteed for a season.

Bobby says "It's better than ever."

If any difficulty in obtaining same write direct to

	2-5	6-11
WHITE SOLE	39/11	49/11
BLACK SOLE	37/6	47/6

BOZEAT BOOT CO. LTD., BOZEAT, NORTHANTS
WHO WILL PUT YOU IN TOUCH WITH NEAREST STOCKIST

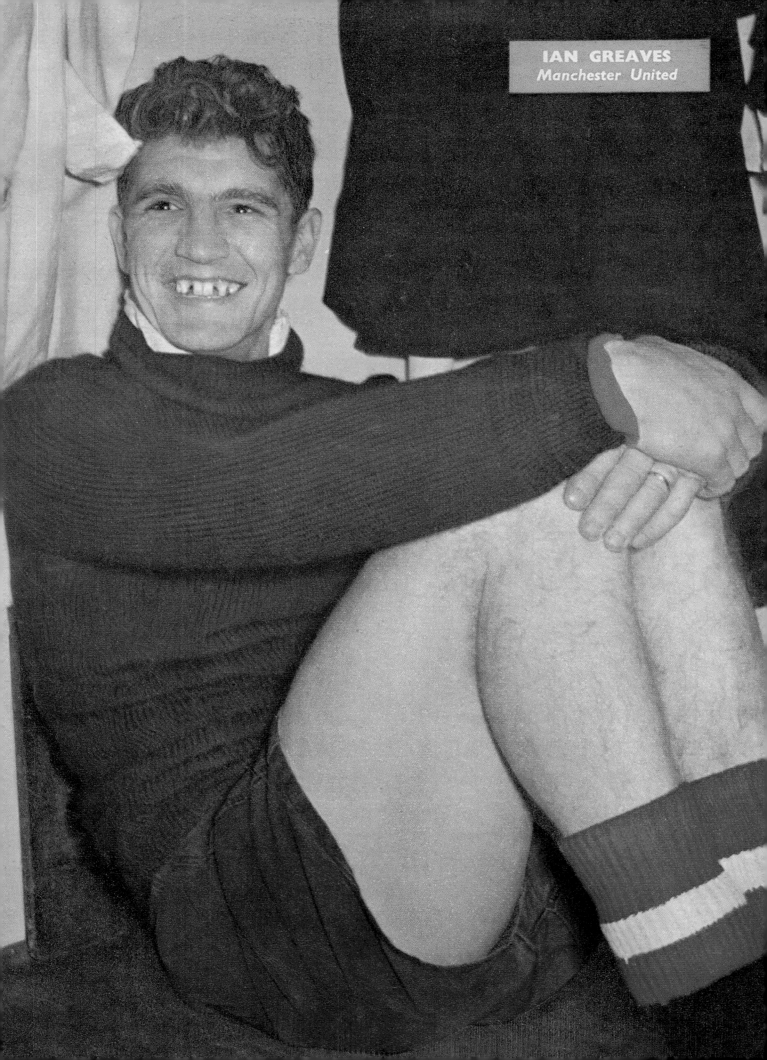

NIGHTMARE!

then came the day when I knew I had a future with the grandest club on earth

by DENNIS VIOLLET
Manchester United

THE Munich air disaster is still too much of a vivid nightmare for me to want to dwell on it. But I have to think of it in the light of what the doctors told me. They said in hospital that I would never play football again.

At the time, the words did not hit me so hard as when I arrived home and began to think of the future.

As my injuries began to heal and my mind became clearer, I began to feel that if I could have only just one game of football I might be able to convince myself whether my desire to carry on was hopeless or not.

After a while, I asked an orthopaedic surgeon in Manchester whether he thought I could play—whether it would be wise to do so.

He gave me the O.K., and so, one evening late last season, when United were booked for Wembley, I was allowed to turn out in a re-arranged First Division game against the Wolves.

A tough test, but I was desperately anxious to try my strength. We were beaten 5—o, but afterwards I felt fit enough and thought I had a fair game,

considering my long lay-off.

Then I began to think I might stand a fair chance of playing at Wembley — which I wanted to do more than anything else.

Because of a troublesome leg injury, I had missed the previous year's Cup Final against Aston Villa, and I badly wanted another chance to gain a Cup winner's medal.

By Wembley-time I had played a few reserve games and three League matches and was confident that I would not let United down in what we all hoped at Old Trafford would be our moment of glory.

You know what happened against Bolton. We could not get going—I felt I had not played well.

Bolton were worthy 2—o winners, and United thus failed to emulate the performance of our Manchester City neighbours in lifting the F.A. Cup after being losing finalists the previous year.

But at least I knew that I still had a future—and part of the great future that must surely lie in store for Manchester United, for me the grandest club on earth.

I was a United fan as a boy, so it is not surprising that I still get a wonderful thrill in turning out in the famous red shirt and in the same position occupied by my schoolboy hero, Stan Pearson.

To me, in those early days, Stan did not seem to have a bad match. I did not dream at the time that I would succeed him.

But, late in the 1953 season, when we were having a poor time in the League, Mr. Matt Busby brought in several young players—Duncan Edwards, Jackie Blanchflower and myself.

We owed a lot to Allenby Chilton, who was then the most experienced player in the side. Allenby had to work tremendously hard at centre-half, with so many immature players around him.

But he was a constant inspiration and held the team together until we found our feet.

He dominated the defence, covered up our mistakes, and found time to encourage each player. Allenby never minced words. He told us on the field exactly what he wanted us to do.

Now he is doing an equally fine job as manager of Grimsby Town, in the Second Division.

I began my Soccer career with Manchester Boys, as an inside-forward, and I was fortunate enough to win five England Schoolboy caps.

As I have grown up with United I have come to admire many of the players against whom I have played.

I think that Tommy Docherty—transferred from Preston to Arsenal early this season—is the best wing-half I have run up against.

And for an inside-forward, give me little Ernie Taylor, who is now our forward-line tactician at Old Trafford. I have long believed he is one of the greatest ball players in post-war Soccer.

Like Chilton before him, Ernie—who was transferred to us from Blackpool immediately after the Munich crash—has been a wonderful inspiration to the new United team.

Bobby Charlton coaches some young hopefuls at the back of his home in Beatrice Street, Ashington, Northumberland.

FROM ASHINGTON'S BACK STREETS...

by BOBBY CHARLTON
MANCHESTER UNITED AND ENGLAND

I HOPE I shan't be accused of being swollen-headed when I say that I am a born footballer. I have been lucky enough to play for England and appear in two Wembley Cup Finals, but the foundation for all that was laid in my home town of Ashington, in Northumberland, where Soccer is more than a game—it is a religion.

Even our womenfolk are daft about football. My mother comes from the famous Milburn footballing family. My second cousin is Jackie Milburn, of Newcastle and England fame. My elder brother, John, is Leeds United's centre-half — following in the Elland Road footsteps of three uncles.

All my relatives live and breathe the game—or so it has always seemed. And ever since I can remember I have had a ball at my feet.

Once it was a grimy little rubber ball which my pals and I would kick about Ashington's streets, collecting other boys as we went, until we had enough to play.

I'm making no apologies for looking back to my boyhood, for it was then that the football which I can truly say was bred in me, began to take seed and bloom.

The plain fact is . . . I could not *help* being a footballer. And I don't suppose any other Ashington boy can help it, either.

The only difference is that I have been lucky enough to get the breaks that some of my schoolboy pals did not.

My cousin, Jackie Milburn, and I seem to be the only members of the family who became forwards—all the older and more venerable footballers were defenders.

My uncles John and George were Leeds United's full-back pair for years. In fact, they were almost an institu-

tion at Elland Road. When George left for Chesterfield, Uncle Jim took his place. Another uncle, Stan, was a full-back at Leicester.

When these uncles came home to Ashington for the occasional week-end, or for the summer, I would 'kid' them to join our kick-about games.

I don't know how it was that I became an inside-forward. I was just picked for that position at school, and in those days it seemed quite natural.

As a ten-year-old, I attended the biggest school in Ashington — Hirst North. So many boys had to be accommodated that the school was divided into two sections, 'A' and 'B'.

Half the school was upstairs, and the other half on the ground floor. So we promptly called ourselves the 'uppies' and the 'doonies' when it came to Soccer warfare.

And what battles we had in the East Northumberland junior schoolboy league. Often our two teams would be winners, or runners-up to each other.

And out of school hours—we played still more football. On any waste ground we could find, and often on Sunday mornings as well as Saturdays.

One of our 'grounds' was close to a bus station.

We would borrow empty oil drums from the garage to use as goalposts. Sometimes we even played on top

▲ 1959–60 Gift Book

of a giant concrete air-raid shelter. Even my mother—a wonderful Soccer enthusiast if ever there was one—would have had a thousand fits if she could have seen us. For that shelter was high, and we could have been badly hurt had we fallen off!

Sometimes—but not very often, because we all preferred to play on Saturday afternoons—we would go into Newcastle to watch the United at St. James's Park.

It cost us 2s. for a day return, and 9d. to get in. It was there that I saw Nat Lofthouse in the first League game I ever attended. How could I have realised that a dozen years later I would play against Nat in the F.A. Cup Final!

I always tried to see Stanley Matthews. It was great to see Stanley perform. And since then I have played against him.

How wonderful it all seems!

For six years I did fairly well in schoolboy Soccer. I played for the district and county boys as a junior, intermediate and senior player. And I managed to achieve the goal of every schoolboy player—a senior England cap.

I appeared against Wales at Wembley, and against Scotland at Leicester. With me in the side were Wilf McGuinness, now an Old Trafford club mate, and Jimmy Melia, of Liverpool.

We are the only members of that England schools side now playing League football. So you see that not all schoolboy internationals make the grade as professionals.

Wilf, by the way, is a great pal of mine. We often go fishing together, when training is over at Old Trafford.

It was before I had actually reached schoolboy international status that the first move was made for me to join Manchester United.

At the start of my last winter at school, Mr. Joe Armstrong, the United scout, came to watch me play.

He approached my parents, of course, and although I am sure they would have preferred me to join Newcastle, they agreed to let me become a Manchester United player when I left school.

Well, then came my international appearances and, of course, the scouts came flocking round to see me—as they do with any promising schoolboy footballer.

United had wanted me to go on to their ground staff right away, but mother wasn't so sure. She insisted that I sign as an amateur, and United agreed to have me apprenticed at an engineering works.

It was something I could fall back on if I failed to make the grade as a professional. It was a wise precaution.

Believe me, there was no guarantee that I would do well, even though I was a schoolboy international.

I soon learned that when I arrived at Old Trafford as a 15-year-old in season 1953-54. There was no chance to become 'big headed'.

I was taken in hand by Mr. Matt Busby, Bert Whalley, Jimmy Murphy and other United stalwarts.

Their advice and coaching in those early days was invaluable. Without it I could not have become the player I am now.

And if I can be said to be in a position to give any advice to ambitious young men who want to make Soccer a career, it is this: *Always be ready and willing to listen to your elders, and keep yourself fit at all times.*

I know that seems to be stating the obvious, but some youngsters seem to think that they can get by on skill alone.

As an inside-forward, I have found it is not so. All the ball control and brilliance in the world is useless if you lack stamina and speed.

... TO THE WEMBLEY TURF

Russian goalkeeper Vladimir Belyayev is beaten by this penalty-kick from Bobby Charlton during an international at Wembley.

If you already have the skill in your feet—and I am assuming that no youngster taken on the books of a League club is without it—the ultimate test of your success is whether or not you can last the pace.

Since I have been a professional I have realised how much easier it is to play top-class Soccer if you are at peak fitness.

Inside-forwards have to do a lot of chasing up and down during a game—it is not all shooting for goal. And unless you can keep going for the full ninety minutes you are letting down your colleagues.

It is not always easy for a youngster to take the lime-light and publicity of success in his stride.

Just before I made my First Division debut for United, at the age of 18, many of the newspapers made no secret of the fact that they considered I should have been in the first team before.

But Mr. Busby wisely let me come along in the reserves and then, one day, almost casually, he put me in against Charlton, at Old Trafford.

Perhaps the reason for United's success in the past has been the kindly, shrewd way in which Mr. Busby has slipped in his youngsters at the right time.

Obviously, United did not earn their name of the 'Busby Babes' for nothing!

In my case, it might have been the 'name' coincidence that decided Mr. Busby to give me my 'blooding' against Charlton.

Footballers' debuts are nearly always nervy affairs in which the youngster scarcely does himself justice. But the luck ran for me that day, and I was fortunate enough to score a hat-trick in our 4—2 win.

Of course, that performance didn't automatically guarantee me a first-team place. Back I went into the reserves, to continue my apprenticeship. I got in the League side only when Tommy Taylor was playing for England.

But I did have one great afternoon of football in the 1957 F.A. Cup semi-final against Birmingham City at Hillsborough, Sheffield.

It so happened that the late David Pegg, who was a Doncaster boy, and myself were great buddies, and we decided that we would really throw into this game everything we had, to try to make names for ourselves.

I had not been told until Thursday that I would be in, and for the next 24 hours I grimly resolved to play my heart out.

It was one of those games which, at the time, seemed so important to David and myself, and it might well have turned out a bitter disappointment.

But it didn't. From the start everything went our way, and I had the delight and honour of scoring the second goal of our convincing 2—0 win which took us through to Wembley.

After the game, David and I hugged each other in glee, shouting, "We did it . . . we did it . . . didn't we?" Our more mature team mates, exultant as they were, must have wondered if success had turned David and me crazy.

But we didn't mind. We both *knew* that we had played as well as we could and things had run for us.

When Dennis Viollet was injured before the Final, I was told I would play against Aston Villa at Wembley. We lost that game 2—1 after Ray Wood, our goalkeeper, had been injured, and we were forced down to ten men for most of the match.

That was disappointing, of course, but not so bad as the following year when, after the Munich disaster, we came back to fight our way through to Wembley again.

And once more we lost. Because we did not play up to form in the match that mattered most, and because, simply enough, Bolton were the better team.

So the less said the better about those two Wembleys that did *not* go my way.

I did have one happy Wembley appearance, however, when I returned to London on May 7, 1958, to play for England against Portugal. I got both the goals in England's 2—1 win.

Then I went to Yugoslavia, but played so badly that I wasn't surprised when, after being selected for England's World Cup party for Sweden, I did not play in a game.

I was most surprised to hear when I returned home that there had been so much Press publicity about my non-inclusion in the England World Cup teams.

And I was equally amazed to learn that so many television critics had considered England had put up a poor show.

Personally, I thought we were very unlucky in several games. We had goals disallowed that would have been winners against Austria and Russia, and I felt we put up a much better performance than many people who stayed at home believed.

I mentioned earlier on that I am really an inside-forward. Frankly, I don't like playing centre-forward, but I am willing to play anywhere the club wants. After all, they do know best.

I served in the Army as a National Serviceman, in the R.A.O.C., and some of the most enjoyable games I can remember came in that period. But I was glad

Mum, seen here helping Bobby Charlton light the candles of his 21st birthday cake, is a great Soccer fan herself.

It takes the hard but happy training seen on the right to keep Bobby on top in a tangle for the ball on the field.

when I finished my 'time'. Often, I have been asked to name the best footballer against whom I have played. That's not a very easy one to answer, because I have not been in the game long enough to form any concrete opinions.

But as far as wing-halves are concerned—and, of course, my immediate opponent has nearly always been the wing-half — I would vote Tommy Docherty, of Arsenal and Scotland, an outstanding performer.

He seldom allows me the chances I like to let fly at goal. And as you all know—I *do* like to shoot as often as possible.

I believe that inside-forwards, no matter what role they are called on to play, either for club or country, must be potential goal-scorers.

With United—for me the finest club in the world— I am a very happy footballer. I spend a lot of my spare time thinking about the game and how I am playing, but I like to relax, like everyone else.

For quite a time now, I have been an enthusiastic record collector, and have two or three hundred discs— mostly of singers. And then there's my fishing—an ideal way to forget football completely for a few hours.

It is too early for me to think of what I'd like to do when my playing days are over. But I believe I would prefer to stay in the game.

Being a professional footballer is a wonderful life. And I hope that any youngster reading this article, who is given the chance to become one, will be as lucky as I have been.

WILF McGUINNESS

Manchester United
and England

TWICE I NEARLY QUIT

TWICE in my life I have thought I would have to quit football. The first time was when I was a scrawny kid of 15, right at the foot of the ladder; the other was two years ago, after the Munich crash, when I had tasted enough success to make the thought of leaving the game even more heartbreaking.

The trouble when I was 15 was my size.

I joined Manchester United straight from school. I was 5 ft. tall and weighed about 10 st.

For a youngster aiming to be a professional footballer, that is small and light!

In fact, when I was with United's juniors they used to play me one week and then rest me the next!

When not playing, I used to watch Jack Rowley, the 'Gunner', and wondered if I would ever be as strong and great as he.

Well, I'm still not in the heavyweight class at 11 st. 10 lb., and 5 ft. 10½ in., but I doubt whether I would have stayed in the game if I had been with any other club than Manchester United.

They persevered with me when the others would have given up.

The late Tom Curry, or 'Tosh', as we knew him, was a wonderful trainer, and with Bill Inglis, his assistant, gave me lots of encouragement.

Then, Jimmy Murphy, United's assistant manager, helped me a lot with my game, and it was he who saved me from the second crisis of my career after the crash.

I was in hospital in Munich, and not feeling too good, when I heard someone behind the screen say: "**Albert Scanlon will never play football again.**"

To this day I don't know who said it, but his opinion certainly shattered my morale.

I decided to ask the next person who came to my bed if it were true.

To my good fortune, the next visitor was Jimmy Murphy, and by the time he had answered my query, I was just about set to play the following week!

It took a little longer than that, of course, but once again Manchester United made it quite clear that no trouble was too much if there was the slightest chance.

But at Old Trafford they don't give up easily and they don't let anyone else do so

Jack Crompton, ex-United goalkeeper, now our trainer, took me in hand at Old Trafford and devised a special training schedule.

He was so successful that my broken right leg, which also had torn ligaments and muscles which had wasted away, **became fatter and stronger than my good leg!**

That is how thorough they are at Old Trafford. But don't think United are a 'soft' club.

No one is picked for the first team on sentiment. No one is certain of his first-team place—as a few of us have found out this season!

We had played only one League match when I was dropped. As I write this article four internationals were dropped into the reserves.

Harry Gregg, Bobby Charlton, Wilf McGuinness and Warren Bradley had to give way to young reserves, David Gaskell, Mark Pearson, Shay Brennan and Alex Dawson.

But there was no moaning, because Manchester United are a fair club—fair to the youngsters as well as the big names.

The shock reminded me of the days just before Munich.

On the Saturday before the crash, there were more internationals in the reserves than in the first team!

Playing against Arsenal at Highbury for the League side were Harry Gregg, Bill Foulkes, Roger Byrne, Duncan Edwards and Tommy Taylor.

But in the reserves at Old Trafford there were five internationals—Ray Wood, Jackie Blanchflower, John Berry, Colin Webster and David Pegg.

I was one of the players to profit from that reorganisation; I went in for David Pegg after spending nearly five years trying to catch him up.

We joined the club together, but while I was battling for muscles, height and weight with the juniors, David was playing for the 'A' or third team.

We were in the Youth team together, David at inside-left and I on the wing, but when I reached the 'A' team David was making his debut in the First Division.

I caught him up in the end and we both knew that the man in form would have the top-team outside-left berth.

It is now cut-throat competition for places at Old Trafford, and that is one of the main reasons why I think you can put Manchester United back on the Soccer map these days.

by ALBERT SCANLON
Manchester United

by SHAY BRENNAN
Manchester United

YOU HAVE TO BE RAZOR-SHARP TO STAY ON TOP AT OLD TRAFFORD

NOTHING keeps a footballer on his toes more than razor-sharp rivalry—the kind we get with Manchester United at Old Trafford.

It is a good thing to have within a club, and I should know better than anyone, for since I joined United's groundstaff, straight from school, I have had to fight for my place against keen opposition.

There has been tremendous rivalry between Freddie Goodwin, Wilf McGuinness and myself for a regular first-team spot.

At one time I thought I had no future at Old Trafford because I went to the club as an inside-forward and, even after Munich, there did not seem to be much chance of superseding Albert Quixall and Bobby Charlton.

I was one of several untried United youngsters who were pitchforked into the team after Munich for that first, memorable fifth round Cup-tie with Sheffield Wednesday when acting manager Jimmy Murphy was struggling to get a side together.

I was on the left-wing for that game, playing before a tense and fanatical crowd of over 60,000 spectators who all wanted us to win.

Before then I had not appeared before a crowd of more than 20,000; that was when I was a member of the United team which won the F.A. Youth Cup a few years back.

And I had never played at outside-left before! What a game it was. I will never forget it. We won 3—0 and I scored two of the goals, my first in big football in what was one of the most vital games in United's long history.

Those two goals are for ever etched on my memory. I scored the first DIRECT *from a corner-kick*—a rather lucky affair, as these shots invariably are.

I tried for an inswinger by hitting the flag kick with my *right* foot. The ball swung in beautifully under the glaring floodlights, was suddenly wafted even farther towards goal by a gust of wind, and curled over the goalkeeper's head and into the net.

In the second-half, the ball came through from our defence to Mark Pearson who switched it quickly to me. I tried a shot, the ball rebounded off a defender and at the second attempt, I rammed it into the Wednesday net for No. 2.

Alex Dawson got our third goal and we were through to the sixth round against all the odds.

After that, some of the Munich survivors, like Dennis Viollet and Bobby Charlton, fit again, came back into the team.

I lost my place before the semi-final and Final—although I *did* play in the semi-final replay against Fulham, at Highbury.

In February, 1959, some twelve months after Munich, I was asked by manager Matt Busby if I would like to have a shot at playing wing-half.

I was glad of the chance to try a new position for, as I have already mentioned, there seemed little scope as a first-team inside-forward or winger just then.

Another chance

I had several useful games in the 'A' and reserve teams in the half-back line, but I had to wait until the last game of the season, at Leicester, before I was given my senior chance.

It was not a particularly good game for me because Leicester were desperate for points to avoid relegation. They beat us 2—1.

In August, 1959, I was back in the reserves. The first team wing-half pair were Freddie Goodwin and Wilf McGuinness, who had played in most of the Cup and League games the previous season.

Then Goodwin was hurt against Chelsea at Old Trafford and I was promoted for the next match, against Newcastle.

I had the tricky George Eastham as my immediate opponent, but I had a surprisingly good game and held my place for the next half-dozen matches.

Then I was injured in the match against Spurs, and Freddie Goodwin came back again. Eventually, he lost form and back I came with another opportunity to stake my claim to a permanent place in the position I now realised was my best.

It was obviously going to be a real tussle between Freddie and myself, with the odds in his favour, for he was by far the more experienced player.

I was in the big Manchester 'derby' game against City, at Maine Road, and played badly. So out I went the next week and again it was Goodwin as No. 4 on the team sheet.

Not until we struck a really bad patch and manager Matt Busby was forced to make drastic team changes did I get another chance.

This time it was at *left-half* in place of Wilf McGuinness.

That was in November, 1959, and I stayed in the team after that, taking part in our Cup run.

By then a new and formidable rival had arrived at Old Trafford—England Under-23 skipper Maurice Setters, who had been transferred from West Bromwich Albion for a big fee.

Although my parents were Irish, I was born in Manchester and attended the St. John's school in Wythenshaw, where I played in the forward line.

When I left school I began to learn the joinery trade and resumed my football with St. John's Old Boys Club in the South Manchester and Wythenshaw League. I was an inside-forward and I managed to net quite a few goals.

When I was playing for the League Representative XI against the Manchester Catholic League, I was spotted by scouts from United and City.

City were first at my home with an offer to join their groundstaff, but I had always been a devout United supporter and so I hung fire and hoped that United would approach me very quickly.

Their representative called to see me only a couple of days after the City scout had been, and when I got the offer to go on the Old Trafford groundstaff, I accepted right away. Of course, I have never regretted it.

As I have said, competition is keen in our club and now we have some likely-looking Irish youngsters on the groundstaff who are going to make us all look to our laurels before very long.

▲ June 1960 | November 1960 ▶

JOHN GILES
Manchester United
and Republic of Ireland

MARK PEARSON

Manchester United

LIVING DOWN THE TEDDY BOY BOGY

SENT OFF!

TWO CAUTIONS!

NAME TAKEN!

SENT OFF AGAIN!

● **I certainly got myself a bad name, but they don't tolerate that sort of reputation at Old Trafford, and I've just had to shake it off.**

THIS season I am happy. In the past twelve months I have been the most worried man in football. Everything seemed to be going wrong, and I was even in fear of my future with Manchester United, the club I love and to whom I owe so much.

The trouble was TROUBLE . . . something I always seemed to be in and which snowballed along until I even dreaded my next game of football.

I was tagged a dirty player, and believe me, when once you are branded like that, it takes some shaking off. It's quite true what they say about giving a dog a bad name!

It all started, really, when I played for United's first team against Burnley at Turf Moor in the 1957-58 season. The match went a bit wild and I was sent off.

United were described as having played like a lot of Teddy boys, and as I was the only one sent off, everyone seemed to assume that I was the worst offender.

I suppose the sideboards I wear helped people to associate me with being a Teddy boy. But then appearances can be deceptive. I still wear my sideburns. A lot of people have wanted me to shave them off. But I like them, and that's the one and only reason I stick to them.

After that Burnley game, things went from bad to worse—playing mostly in the reserves, I had two cautions and then had my name taken.

▲ 1960–61 Gift Book

BOBBY CHARLTON . . . I was happy to be his "stand-in".

not expect to go on indefinitely getting reprieves.

So I tried even harder to stay on the right side of the law. Mr Busby told me I must just take any provocation, appeal to the referee if necessary, but certainly not take the law into my own hands.

Now I think I can honestly claim to have laid that 'Teddy Boy' bogy. I steered clear of anything serious in 1959-60, and I look ahead confidently once again.

I am enjoying my football once more, and if I ever run into trouble with a referee again, it will be an isolated instance and the kind of thing that can happen to any player any time.

Now I hope to do justice to my early schoolboy football which first attracted Manchester United's scouts. I captained my school team in my home village of Ridgeway near Sheffield.

★ ★ ★

I also captained Derbyshire boys, played for England schoolboys four times and won an English youth cap.

I joined United's ground staff straight from school —and have never regretted it for a moment since. For one thing, I doubt whether any other top club in the country would have been so patient with me.

I am usually Bobby Charlton's stand-in, and although I had quite a number of First Division games after the Munich crash, I only had three senior side appearances in 1958-59.

On each occasion it was because Bobby was injured or away playing for England. Last season, however, I hit a highspot . . . I actually kept Bobby out of the team on form for three matches!

Then, for a while I played inside to Bobby when he was switched to the left-wing last March.

Our first game as left-wing partners was marked by a fine success over Nottingham Forest when Bobby scored twice in our 3-1 win. I enjoyed this game, for Bobby and I seemed to click right from the start.

Shortly afterwards in the October of 1958, I was sent off for the second time in my career. I was only 18, far too young to be building up a crime sheet like that.

I was suspended, and I was really worried. I thought Mr. Busby's patience must come to an end.

To my good fortune, our manager stood by me once again. Don't think he was condoning my conduct. Several times he had read the riot act to me, and I knew I was only being allowed to stay on at Old Trafford because of his patience and understanding.

It made me very happy and grateful to learn that Leyton Orient had made a bid for me and the 'Boss' had turned it down.

★ ★ ★

This was like a vote of confidence in me, and it bucked me up no end when I read in a local Manchester paper this quote from Mr. Busby:

"He is a great player and will be greater when he learns to curb his occasional outbursts. If he wants to take his chance he has a future at Old Trafford, and I want him here."

I had always tried to play the game on the field. I think I suffered in the end from older players trying to provoke me, and after my first spot of bother, I think some referees had me marked down as a trouble-maker and came gunning for me at the first opportunity.

But 'dirty' players are not tolerated at Old Trafford, and I knew that however many excuses I had, I could

MATT BUSBY . . . he had faith in me.

A moment in time...

FEBRUARY 19, 1958. The silent minute, when 59,848 people at Old Trafford, Manchester, mourned the footballers who had been killed on the Munich Airport 13 days earlier, seemed more like a year. It was almost possible to hear their tears drop. On the pitch were the players of Sheffield Wednesday and a strange assortment labelled Manchester United.

As the silence broke, the sides were lined up. The referee looked around, extended his left arm, waved them on with his right as if he were a traffic policeman, and blew his whistle. A postponed fifth round Cup match was on its way.

Within a few seconds it had become a rip-roaring clash, with all the elements associated with the scramble for the Cup. Manchester United won by three clear goals; Sheffield Wednesday paid the compliment of making them go all the way to success.

The United forwards, some of them mere boys, thrown into this cauldron of human drama and emotions, played like men possessed. The defence was a rock. At precisely 7.58 p.m., Seamus Brennan, a 19-year-old inside-forward from the great Johnny Carey's old club in Dublin, shot the first goal.

"As the ball came near to goal it swerved incredibly in the mist and the breeze," we recorded at the time. In front of us, in the great grandstand, a woman crossed herself and said: "Perhaps one of them gave it a push."

At the end, among the unrestrained joy of the tremendous crowd, Jimmy Murphy, stand-in for the famous Matt Busby, allowed his tears to flow without shame. In the crowd was a girl, wearing one of those long scarves on which are inscribed the names of the players. Against those who were no longer with us she had sewn a small black square. She, too, made no effort to restrain her tears.

Soccer history was moving forward again. It had been shattered and ground to a standstill at the end of that Munich runway. In that cold and misty February evening were the past, the present, the future, the beginning and the end, tragedy and triumph. The people who were *not* there overshadowed the occasion. It was the saddest, the most poignant and the most wonderful match of all the games I have watched.

Among those we missed in this match were Roger Byrne, the former captain, Eddie Colman, David Pegg, Geoffrey Bent, Tommy Taylor, the England centre-forward, Mark Jones and Bill Whelan, all killed outright in the crash. And Duncan Edwards, who would have become one of the all-time greats, who died in the hospital later on.

His former schoolmaster said: "He was the quiet boy, who always came to school with a tennis ball in his pocket, and controlled it perfectly on the asphalt playground."

Among those not present was Matt Busby, the manager, the architect and creator of that great team, who lay between life and death in the great modern hospital at Munich. Ward-sister Erna Straub looked the other way as, one by one, in stints of five minutes, Ray Wood, Bert Scanlon, Dennis

by ALAN HOVE

Viollet and Ken Morgans slid from their beds and along to the white-painted dispensing room.

A kick-by-kick account of the game was being relayed. Duncan Edwards, Bobby Charlton, Jackie Blanchflower and Johnny Berry were too ill to know what was going on. Of the established team, only Harry Gregg, the Irish international goalkeeper and Bill Foulkes, the right-back, newly appointed captain, played against Sheffield Wednesday.

The other Irishman, Brennan, scored the second goal and the centre-forward Dawson, known to his friends as the Dreadnought, scored the third.

★   ★   ★

Now the incredible. On another green pitch, early in May, and this time at Wembley Stadium, a small bunch of players stood for just a minute while Bolton Wanderers received the F.A. Cup and the medals which go to the winners.

Those who waited were this amazing Manchester United new team who, by beating West Bromwich Albion 1—0, and Fulham, at Highbury 5—3 in the semi-final, on each occasion after a replay, had got into the Final for the second successive season. And been beaten.

★   ★   ★

February 6, 1958. A minute before half-past-four, thousands of people in Britain tuned in to the B.B.C. to hear the latest entry in Mrs. Dale's diary. They heard, in the one-minute news summary, how disaster had struck the world famous football team.

I was one of them, in my flat at Hove, Sussex. In a neat, semi-detached house in Chorlton, Mrs. Harry Gregg, wife of the goalkeeper, was saying comforting words to Mrs. Jackie Blanchflower. Mavis Gregg had heard that her husband was a survivor. Jean Blanchflower had heard nothing of hers.

As Mrs. Gregg arrived, so came the news that Jackie was also safe. "I don't care if he never plays again, so long as he is all right," said Mrs. Blanchflower, prophetically.

In many places of worship, and in their hearts, the people of Manchester remembered their players—and officials, Herbert Whalley, Walter Crickmer and Tom Curry—who had gone. In the beautiful church of St. Bride, in Fleet Street, bombed in the war and arising from the ashes, we of the Press also remembered our colleagues and pals— Alf Clarke (*Manchester Evening Chronicle*), Don Davies (*Guardian*), George Follows (*Herald*), Tom Jackson (*Manchester Evening News*), Archie Ledbrooke (*Mirror*), Henry Rose (*Express*), Eric Thompson (*Mail*) and Frank Swift (*News of the World*).

As the mixed choir sang "I will lift up mine eyes unto the Hills", and the congregation "Swift to its close . . ." there was for me, anyhow, the eerie feeling that spirits were floating in the rafters.

How Alf Clarke, who talked of Manchester United as "We", Henry Rose, who had a regular session signing autographs for the fans, Archie Ledbrooke, always ready for a debate, quietly humorous Eric Thompson, George Follows of the happy grin, eager Tom Jackson and Don Davies, pipe and all, would have thrilled to the epic against Sheffield Wednesday and that Cup Final.

These were the craftsmen, the cream of their profession. The giant Elizabethan, called the "Lord Burghley", lurching along that Munich runway, had been the means to their end.

The game, like the show it is, goes on. Time mellows and soothes. Matt Busby is back on the job. Ray Wood is with Huddersfield Town. Jackie Blanchflower, as said, and the streaking outside-right Johnny Berry never played again.

Albert Scanlon has moved to Newcastle, Ken Morgans is now with Swansea, but United's attack is still graced by the cultured football of Dennis Viollet.

▲ September 1961

God is with us for our Captain.

The memory of a fine young sportsman is forever commemorated in St. Francis Church, Dudley, Worcestershire. There, two stained glass windows—this is one of them—have been installed in tribute to the late Duncan Edwards, the modest local boy who reached sporting fame with Manchester United and England, and who died after the tragic crash at Munich of the plane carrying Manchester United from Yugoslavia, in 1958.

I became a centre-forward and GOALKEEPER by ACCIDENT!

This is Harry Gregg in action . . . . Alex Dawson has no desire to copy him.

TWO matches, on different Soccer levels, and played six years apart, will always be of special significance to me whenever I look back on my football career. Each time I was wearing the famous colours of Manchester United.

No. 1 was a fourth-team game against Oldham Athletic. I was then an outside-right and, at 15, dreaming of becoming a Matthews, a Finney or—because I am a Scot—a Gordon Smith.

I had no vision of donning the No. 9 shirt worn by such famous Old Trafford figures as Jack Rowley and the late Tom Taylor. But fate took a hand before a handful of spectators that afternoon.

At centre-forward was Kenny Morgans—still a member of United's staff—and when he took a nasty knock, our coach, the late Bert Whalley, signalled me to move to the centre. I hit a hat-trick — and have been on the goal trail ever since.

No. 2 was in January, 1961, in our "classic" with Championship-chasing Spurs. But that is no happy hat-trick memory, because throughout the second-half I was busy saving goals and not trying to score them!

It was quite a shock when I was asked to take over "between the sticks" when Harry Gregg damaged a shoulder. Fortunately, I did reasonably well before a record crowd of 65,295—a bit different from when I made that other positional switch against Oldham!

I was born in Aberdeen, of Scottish parents, and stayed on the Scots side of the border until I was eleven.

My father was, and is, a trawlerman. He was fishing out of Hull! so much that the family decided to set up house on the Yorkshire coast. That, too, was a lucky move for me.

I had always been keen on Soccer, but as a wing-half. I played at left-half for my school and at inside-forward and on the wing for Hull Boys' team. But I never wore the No. 9 jersey.

I had one game with the county schools side, a number of international trial matches—and four full caps from England! My international appearances were all at outside-right.

But I regard that Oldham game as the turning point in my career. I became a bustling, hustling leader by accident—that accident to slightly-built Kenny Morgans!

And you imagine how much I owe to the late Bert Whalley—like lovable, lively Tommy Taylor, a victim of the air disaster at Munich in February, 1958, Bert was a first-class coach and friend.

. . . and you can keep the job in goal . . .

says **ALEX DAWSON Manchester United**

Bert had been a centre-half — his playing career ended because of eye trouble just after the war — and he spent many anxious hours with me, for who better than a pivot to teach a centre-forward all the tricks of the trade?

Now, because I played in goal against Tottenham and because I have said that match was a landmark in my store of memories, don't get the idea that I fancy myself as a Harry Gregg, a Ron Springett, or a Bert Trautmann. Far from it . . .

I was really shaky at the thought of facing Bobby Smith and company. It was my public debut as a goal-keeper and it seemed a far cry from the practice pitch and those lighthearted five-a-sides when Harry and I switched jobs just for a lark!

This was the real thing, but the rest of the lads hit a new peak in revealing the teamwork for which every United side is famous.

They covered me magnificently and even lucky saves brought a pat on the back from skipper Maurice Setters and a word or two of encouragement from Noel Cantwell and Bill Foulkes.

▲ 1961–62 Gift Book

Charles Buchan's
FOOTBALL
MONTHLY

JUNE 1962

1/6
Overseas price 2/-
Forces overseas 1/6

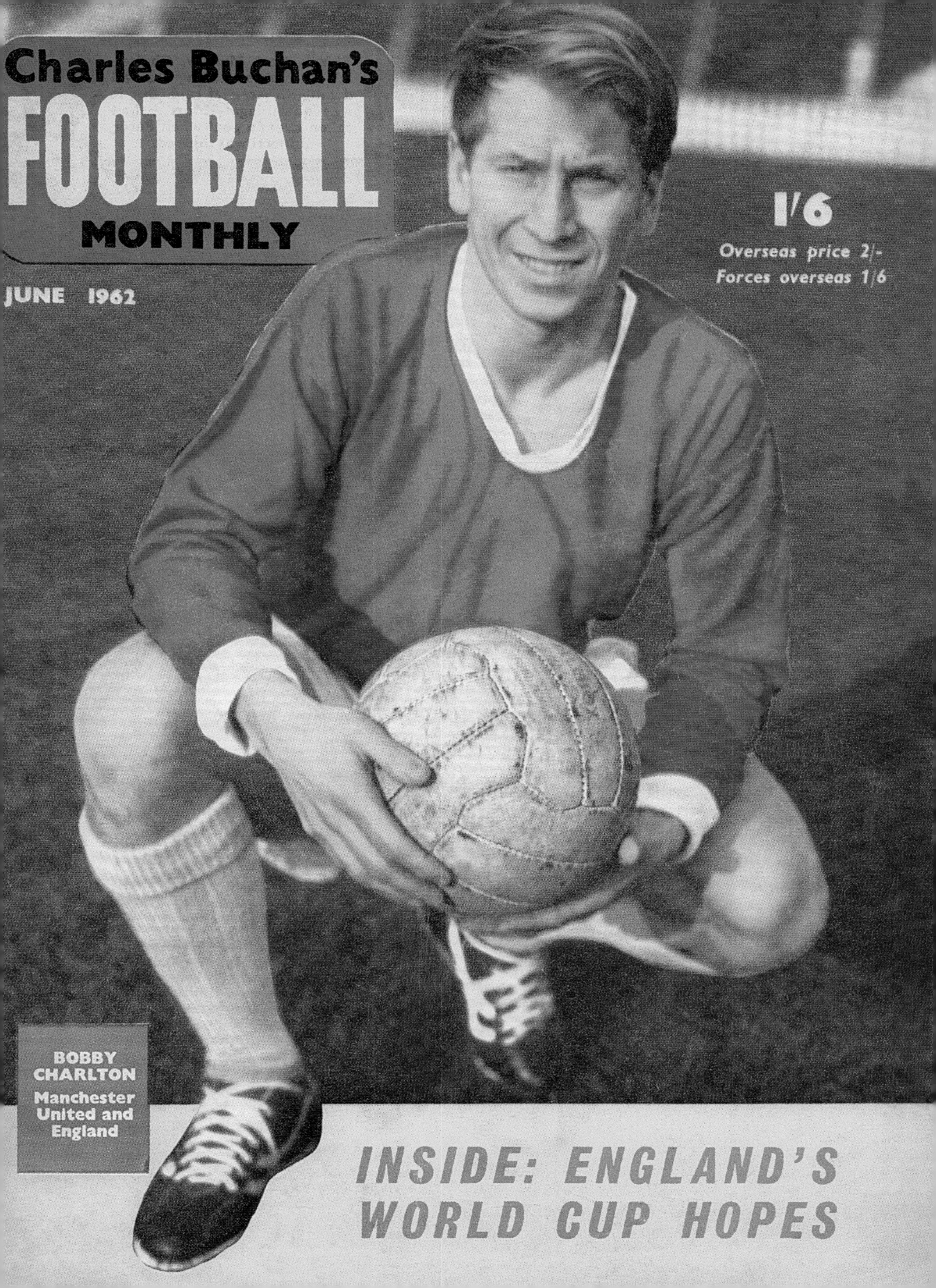

BOBBY
CHARLTON
Manchester
United and
England

*INSIDE: ENGLAND'S
WORLD CUP HOPES*

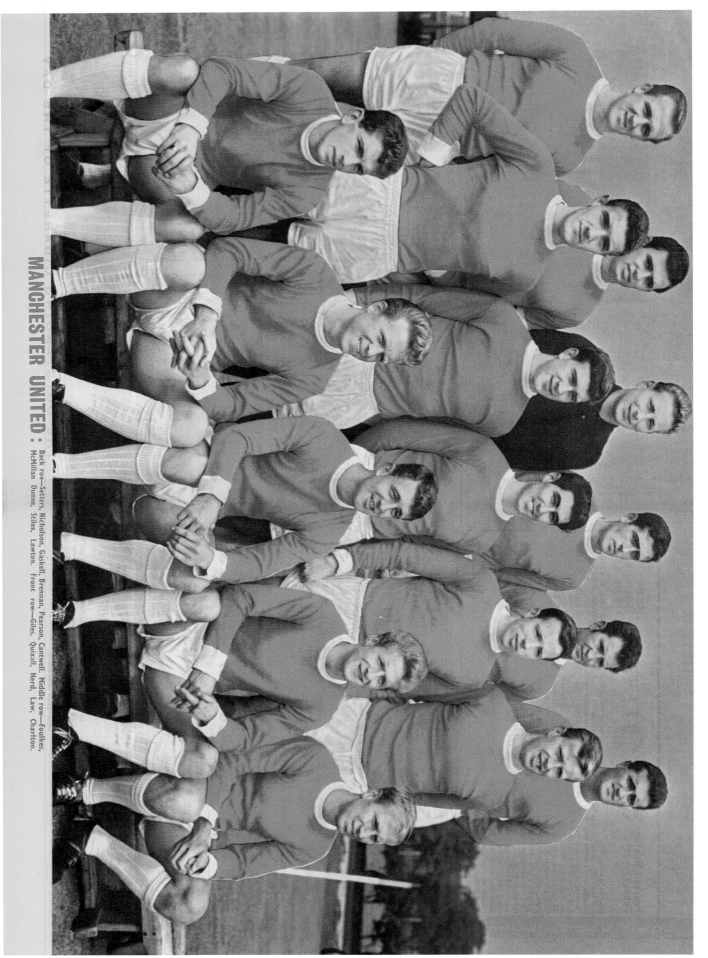

MANCHESTER UNITED : Back row—Setters, Nicholson, Gaskell, Brennan, Pearson, Cantwell. Middle row—Foulkes, McMillan Dunne, Stiles, Lawton. Front row—Giles, Quixall, Herd, Law, Charlton.

▲ February 1963

David Herd flings up his arms and yells with glee as he scores Manchester United's second goal in the Cup Final against Leicester City (top). Another arm-raising act (below), by Denis Law. But this time it was with exasperation for his header had come off a post and into the ready hands of Gordon Banks.

▲ August 1963

BLACK SATURDAY

Saturday, November 16, 1963, was a black day for the so-called sporting spirit of English footballers and crowds.

It was the day when Denis Law (above), of Manchester United and Scotland—Britain's most expensive and talented player—was sent off at Villa Park.

It was the day when this scene (below) was snapped at Elland Road, during the match between Leeds and Preston when there were so many scuffles that the referee had to call ALL players together to read the riot act to them.

Elsewhere, other players were sent off, crowds invaded pitches, bottles and other missiles were thrown.

When will they ever learn? When will they ever learn?

▲ January 1964 | June 1966 ▶

DENIS LAW
Manchester United

CHARLES BUCHAN'S
FOOTBALL
MONTHLY

CHARLES BUCHAN'S

The World's Greatest Soccer Magazine

MAY, 1964

2/-

OVERSEAS PRICE 2
FORCES OVERSEA
2/-

CUP FINAL SOUVENIR

The Choice of Champions

UMBRO

Some of the triumphant Manchester United team in their UMBRO jerseys, shorts and hose.

WIN AGAIN AT WEMBLEY FOR THE FIFTH CONSECUTIVE TIME

*Note also the **adidas** boots, the original make with the three stripes

Club Secretaries are invited to write for the 1963 Umbrochure direct to Humphreys Bros. Ltd., P.O. Box No. 5, Umbro Hse., Wilmslow, Cheshire

▲ September 1963

PANIC!

I couldn't sleep
... I couldn't eat

by DAVID SADLER
Manchester United

were trips to Switzerland, Holland, Spain, the Canary Islands and northern France, so my first season was a memorable one —far more than I had ever hoped for.

When I joined Manchester United 19 months ago, I soon realised I knew nothing about football. But now I have gained more experience than at any other time in my life—and I am still serving my apprenticeship!

It has not taken me long to learn that to get anywhere in football, 99 per cent is not enough—you have to dedicate yourself and devote everything to the game.

I have been a very lucky young man so far, all the lucky breaks have swung my way. This season I am not counting on nearly so many first-team games, although you can be sure I shall be doing everything I can to challenge David Herd for the centre-forward place.

Professional football has not changed me much. Obviously, the money is a contrast to what I used to earn in the bank where I worked in Maidstone, Kent. And travel is often first-class. Also, I can jump in a taxi when I feel like it; eat at a good restaurant; manage more than one visit to a cinema or theatre a week.

But I have settled down pretty well in Manchester and have made some firm friends, inside and outside the club. The other players helped me to fit in—and also let me stand on my own feet. I have had a lot of help from Noel Cantwell and Maurice Setters (who is now with Stoke).

To think that two years ago I had scarcely been out of Yalding! That is my home, a small, picturesque village just outside Maidstone. The only time it gets into the news is when the winter rains flood the river!

Such a lot has happened to me so quickly. It seems no time at all since I was playing for my school side, Maidstone Technical, and Maidstone and Kent boys' representative teams. I got a place in an England schoolboy trial, but I never made the full team.

It was a great thrill when I was invited to join my local amateur club, Maidstone United, who play in the Isthmian League.

I finished that season as the club's top scorer with 17 goals in 22 games, but Maidstone ended bottom of the League.

The next season was an even bigger success for me. I was 16½ when I was picked to play for England amateurs against Ireland, and by that time the League scouts were coming after me.

England picked me a second time, against Wales, and shortly afterwards I signed amateur forms for Manchester United. In February of that season I signed professional forms.

It was a difficult decision, but I made it. I am sure it was the right one.

NEVER had I felt so nervous! I could not sleep or eat normally. I was almost in a state of panic. The Saturday ahead completely occupied my thoughts.

That was my reaction to the news that I had been picked to play my first game for Manchester United, my boyhood idols, for their opening League game last season, against Sheffield Wednesday.

I shall always remember that occasion. After a training session in the club gym, the boss, Mr. Matt Busby, announced the team. To my utter amazement he read out my name. I could not believe it!

But when the time came and the match got under way at Hillsborough I tried to forget the big occasion and the 32,000 crowd, and concentrate on my football. There were two or three other players of my age making their debut in the side, and that helped me to feel more at ease. And although I found it hard work up against the ex-England pivot, Peter Swan, he was fair and I had no complaints.

It was a good game and we drew 3-3. I did not score, but I felt quite happy at having a hand in one of Bobby Charlton's two goals.

I was even happier when I learned I was keeping my place for the next game, against Ipswich Town.

I played 12 League games on the trot, and a European Cup-tie against the Dutch side, Wilhem.

In all I was picked for more than 20 first-team games; I won a medal with the Junior World Cup side; I collected a winner's plaque when Manchester beat Swindon Town in the F.A. Youth Cup Final. At the age of 18, I had become one of the famous "Busby Babes". There

▲ January 1965

Flying high!

Bobby Charlton, of Manchester United, and Jim Furnell, of Arsenal, jump to it. That's Denis Law whose face is blotted out by Furnell's left foot.

▲ 1964–65 Giftbook

DEAR SIR

you write to us

Yes or No?

I THINK Manchester United's George Best, the young Irish winger, bears a striking resemblance to the American singer, Gene Pitney.

N. POWELL,
3, Bunes Road, Gt. Cornard,
Sudbury, Suffolk.

THINGS THEY SAY

BECAUSE I was born with fair hair and a face something like a cross between Tommy Steele and Danny Kaye people may think that I'm incapable of being down in the dumps.

They don't know me.

I am being very serious indeed when I say that my suspension last season was sheer disaster for me. What made it worse was that I knew I deserved to be suspended.

Denis Law, Manchester United, to Clive Toye, "Daily Express".

Knight Matt!

IT is high time somebody else from football joined Sir Stanley Matthews as a Knight. The person who immediately springs to mind is Matt Busby.

He has managed a top club for over 20 years, taken them to countless honours, including four Cup Finals, four League titles, three F.A. Charity Shield wins, six F.A. Youth Cup victories and three European Cup semi-finals.

Moreover, when the Munich disaster is taken into account, even rival supporters at Liverpool and Manchester City must wonder why Mr. Busby has only a C.B.E.

Can Sir Ralph Richardson, Sir Michael Redgrave, Sir Donald Wolfit, Sir Felix Aylmer and Sir Laurence Olivier, great actors as they are, claim to have achieved so much or entertained so many?

K. J. BARRATT,
14, Chesham Ave., Flixton,
Nr. Manchester.

Selected from 1963–65

DEAR SIR

you write to us

Yes or No?

HOW about showing pictures of George Best and Gene Pitney, the pop singer? I think they are very much alike.

MISS ANN GILL.
29, Bridge End, Egremont, Cumberland.

(More than a hundred letters were received pointing out this particular "double". Now judge for yourselves . . . Best on the left.)

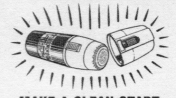
March 1965 ▶

GEORGE BEST
Manchester United

There are two policemen in this lot (see if you can find them). They were caught in the delirious surge of fans when Manchester United won last season's League Championship. Below, Matt Busby celebrates.

HAPPY AND VICTORIOUS!

▲ June 1965

You pick the words—they'll probably fit!
This is Pat Dunne, Manchester United
goalkeeper, after letting in a Spurs goal.

▲ December 1965

HALF-A-MILLION

An impression of Old Trafford's new stand.

Getting ready for the World Cup !

In last month's issue, Eric Taylor, general manager and secretary of Sheffield Wednesday, wrote of the preparations his club are making for the World Cup Finals, to be held in England next year.

Now, Les Olive, secretary of Manchester United, writes of the plans of his club to impress our visitors. They include a £300,000 new stand . . . waiters . . . carpets . . . special boxes . . . lifts . . . all mod. con.—to impress with the best.

BY the time July, 1966, and the World Cup, comes around, we at Old Trafford will have spent three years on preparations for our part in this event.

We are proud that we were chosen by the Football Association to stage World Cup games, and we intend to do everything possible to uphold the prestige of Manchester—and to make our contribution worthy of the North West. My club want to help to make this event a most memorable one, for the World Cup is not likely to be staged again in England for a long time.

Top of our list of ground improvements is the erection of a magnificent cantilever stand which will undoubtedly set a new standard of comfort in every possible way.

This stand has been in mind for some time, but the World Cup series has prompted the club to press forward sooner than expected—even at the cost of reducing our ground capacity during the time of building.

Now almost completed (the main part will be ready for the start of the 1965-66 season!) it will finally accommodate 10,000 fans in specially designed tip-up chairs with curved seats and backs, and 10,000 standing under cover.

One new and interesting feature will be the installation of 34 private boxes each of which will hold six people.

These have been taken up by business houses in the city to entertain their clients in the best possible surroundings—a sort of Soccer-Ascot if you like.

There will be a waiter-service available for refreshments, and a private lift will transfer spectators from ground level to the boxes which will be approached via a luxuriously-carpeted lounge. The boxes will be heated, and high-class refreshment bars will be installed.

When all is done it will indeed be a far cry from the old-time conception of the football fan standing in the open in all kinds of weather, shouting himself hoarse.

In fact, it will be the equal of anything that the world Soccer-traveller will find no matter where he goes.

But, of course, there is much more to World Cup facilities than one new stand—

▲ September 1965

(and more!)

by LES OLIVE
secretary of Manchester United

has a lot of experience in football. They will have the assistance of representatives of G.P.O., Thos. Cook & Sons (travel agents), their own Press and public relations officer, representatives of the local government and different organisations in the city.

The object of this committee is to ensure that visitors to Manchester, especially foreign visitors, should leave with the best possible impression.

Everyone here is on trial

Hotel accommodation, restaurants, entertainment facilities, transport, car-parking arrangements, stores and shops, and the people of the city will all have a part to play in making our visitors feel welcome.

Many foreigners will be taking their annual holiday in Britain and combining it with watching the championship matches.

They will tour the country between games, and the treatment they receive is of the utmost importance. Everyone in the area will be on trial—even the man or woman in the street, who may be stopped and asked for information.

You will see that the task of this committee is formidable and it is hoped that the aid of the civic authorities, leading commercial interests, Press representatives, and all local bodies will give their support in order that justice to our city can be done.

We look forward to the challenge of this event, to presenting the international teams playing for this great championship, and to bringing Soccer stars and personalities to Old Trafford for the benefit not only of our own supporters, but of football followers in the North-West.

It is our privilege to do this and we shall do all in our power to make the World Cup games a huge success.

no matter how large or luxurious. When completed, ours will have cost more than £300,000 but by 1966 we will have spent, in all, more than £500,000 over the past 15 years on improvements at Old Trafford.

Two corner paddocks have been rebuilt and cover has been erected behind the Stretford goal. Our main stand (destroyed by enemy war-time action), has been rebuilt and its design will prove a tremendous boon in accommodating visiting radio, television, and Press representatives.

We will have to remove seats to extend the Press box to take at least 400 Soccer writers, and we shall have to provide them with working and rest rooms.

We will require at least 300 telephone lines, a communications room, radio and TV interview rooms, and platforms for TV and film cameras which will show pictures of the matches in all parts of the world.

Luckily, we have sufficient space in which to erect these temporary structures on the first-floor level underneath our "A" and "D" stands.

Our time-table is set, our plans are ready, and we shall do our best to ensure that Manchester United offer nothing but the best in comfort and facilities at a time when the eyes of the world will be on Britain.

A liaison committee has been formed under the chairmanship of Mr. S. T. Pilkington (vice-president of the Lancashire Football Association). The secretary is Mr. J. M. Howarth (another vice-president of the Lancashire Football Association). Each

"Darling, wouldn't it be nice to spend a few days in Sheffield with your mother in July?"

GEORGE BEST

of Manchester United

tells what it is like to be...

GEORGE BEST ... with trimmings.

PLAYING WITH A GENIUS

... DENIS LAW (left)

THE more I hear and read that "Denis Law kids his team-mates as much as the opposition", the more I laugh. It is a load of rubbish!

Denis is constantly roving around. But when he's on the ball you know that something is going to happen.

He releases the ball in a flash. He may stop first, look around, move quickly forward. He may beat one man or even two. You know he's going to pass—but when? You have to be ready, for he won't give you the ball unless you are in a better position than he is.

That, probably, is why he is accused of selfishness—which

▲ 1965–66 Gift Book

is ridiculous. His one object is to see the ball in the opposing team's net and if any colleague is more likely than he to score—then Denis won't hang on.

I am often asked if I find it difficult playing alongside a star of his calibre. The answer is NO!

He wanders from the inside-left position, and at first I found it a bit disconcerting that my partner wasn't always alongside me. But that's First Division football—you just have to use your brains more often!

I quickly found that out when I was pitch-forked into the League side on Boxing Day, 1963. I had been allowed to travel to my home in Belfast for the Christmas holidays, and was settling down to enjoy the festivities, when I got a telegram telling me to report to Old Trafford at once.

I took the first 'plane, hurried to the ground and found that I had been chosen to play against Burnley at outside-left—although I was an inside-forward.

Since that Boxing Day game I have held on to the left-wing position—and I give my dad the credit for that. He always impressed me, a natural right-footer, that I should learn to use my left foot as much as possible.

I'm glad, too, that I had the sense to listen to him. But this doesn't alter the fact that I still want to be at inside-right. I like to be where the game is thickest. I know it is rougher in the middle, I know there is more room to work on the wing. But I still want to get back into an inside position.

I am often asked which was my best game. Well, I got the biggest kicks out of the semi-final and the final of the F.A. Youth Cup 1963-64, which United won.

The semi-final consisted of two legs against Manchester City. We won at Old Trafford 4—1 and at Maine Road 4—3. I am an Irishman, with no Manchester ties, but at Old Trafford, wherever we come from, our No. 1 enemy is Manchester City. We love to lick them. They feel the same about us!

My best League game was when we played Chelsea at Stamford Bridge in September last year. Chelsea hadn't been beaten at home—they were top of the League—and we beat them 2—0.

There was a big crowd . . . the atmosphere was terrific. And the whole United side hit form that day. I played well! —I just couldn't help it in that company. It was a great day for all of us.

But even greater was the night of Monday, April 26, last . . . when United beat Arsenal 3—1 and won the League title. True, we scraped home only by goal average, but what a wonderful scrap it had been with Leeds and Chelsea!

We had seemed to be the outsiders, and it was a great blow to us when Leeds shot us out of the Cup. But the boys kept going in grand style and the chance was really there when we pipped Leeds at Elland Road.

So to that Monday evening, with Arsenal to beat to make sure. I've never seen such scenes when the final whistle went and the title was ours. It was chaotic at the end with fans invading the pitch. I've never heard such a din. I didn't know whether to laugh or cry. I probably did both!

I'm still a teenager in a man's world, and learning—learning for instance, that if I do anything wrong there is one man who will state his case in no uncertain terms —Denis Law.

And when Denis tells you—you remain told!

GEORGE COHEN (above) takes the ball from Best during a Fulham-Manchester United match. Below, BEST—the one with the Beatle-style haircut—when playing for Ireland, robs Gordon Milne, of England.

PAT CRERAND
Manchester Untd.

DENIS LAW

YOU LIKE HIM...
YOU HATE HIM...
—HE CAME OUT NO. 1

DENIS LAW is back on top! Our readers made him No. 1 in their Top Ten. So Denis the Menace, top of the poll in 1963, second to Bobby Moore last year, has again finished in front.

In a record return, the idol of Old Trafford polled 620 votes. At No. 2 Moore pulled in 593, and Bobby Charlton, Law's club-mate, was third with 581.

Here's how their nearest rivals fared: 4, Jackie Charlton (Leeds), 573; 5, Jimmy Greaves (Spurs), 554; 6, Bobby Collins (Leeds), 551; 7, Peter Thompson (Liverpool), 547; 8, Nobby Stiles (Man. Utd.), 539; 9, Ron Yeats (Liverpool), 528; 10, Stan Anderson (Newcastle), 511.

Players who had many votes without quite making the Top Ten were Jimmy Dickinson, Billy Bremner, Terry Venables, Alick Jeffrey, Bryan Douglas, Ray Wilson, Terry Paine, Alan Ball, Ron Flowers and Roger Hunt. Now for some of YOUR views about it all . . .

NO. 1, Denis Law, Britain's greatest player; 2, Bobby Charlton, hardest shot in the game; 3, Jimmy Greaves, ace-poacher; 4, Bobby Moore, giant in defence for West Ham and England; 5, Jackie Charlton, England's No. 5 at long last; 6, Peter Thompson, England's "Garrincha"; 7, John Connelly, great winger, fast and direct; 8, George Best, greatest prospect for years; 9, Robin Stubbs, the only "class" player in the Fourth Division; 10, Alick Jeffrey for an amazing come-back.

S. M. FRAZIER,
3, Lower Polsham Road,
Paignton, Devon.

NO. 1, Bobby Charlton, for consistent world-class play. 2, Tommy Smith, a meteoric rise to fame; 3, Nobby Stiles, solidity to England's defence; 4, Bobby Collins, inspired leadership for Leeds; 5, John Sissons, has added power to his speed; 6, Fred Pickering, has justified his huge fee; 7, Tony Dunne, his speed and class a joy to watch; 8, Ron Flowers, tireless worker for a poor team; 9, Gary Sprake, great last line of defence; 10, Chris Lawler, has found his best position.

BRIAN DANIELS,
50, Burleigh Road, Penn Fields,
Wolverhampton.

MY selection is as follows: 1, Jim Iley, most skilful and consistent wing-half; 2, Bobby Moore, for successful season as England's captain; 3, Jack Charlton, proved he is no "has been"; 4, Bill Stevenson, for a great display in Final at Wembley; 5, Bobby Collins, for his great come-back with Scotland; 6, Peter Thompson, easily the best left-winger in game today; 7, Stan Anderson, Newcastle's gain, Sunderland's loss; 8, Joe Kiernan, for a successful season with "shock team", Northampton; 9, Peter McConnell, for his captaincy of promoted Carlisle; 10, Alick Jeffrey, for dropping hints to First Division managers with his goal-scoring feats in the Fourth Division.

FRANK WATSON,
222, Newburn Road, Throckley,
Newcastle-upon-Tyne.

BOBBY MOORE

BOBBY CHARLTON

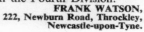

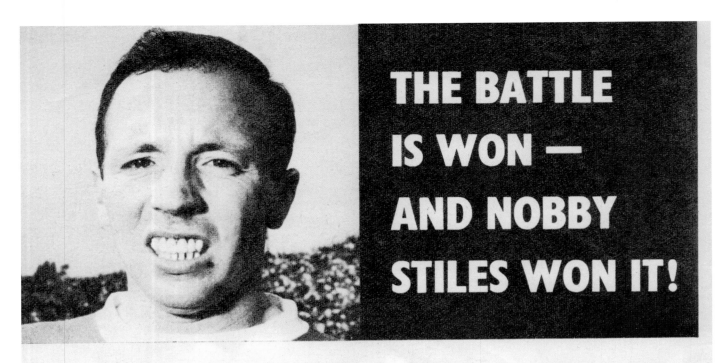

THE BATTLE IS WON — AND NOBBY STILES WON IT!

It was a fight to succeed in top-class company . . . and there were times of despair. But Nobby Stiles, of Manchester United, won through. Here is an appreciation of him.

SOCIALLY, he's as nice a guy as you could ever wish to meet, but when he pulls on a football jersey and goes onto the field, then he's a tiger. That's Nobby Stiles, wing-half of Manchester United and England.

Although he won't be 24 for a few months yet, Nobby has been at Old Trafford for close on 10 years. And if ever a player has had to battle to win recognition, that player is Stiles.

When Manchester United were crippled by the Munich disaster eight years ago, the name of Nobby Stiles was virtually unknown. It wasn't long before Bobby Charlton became a national Soccer idol; before Shay Brennan hit the headlines as a play-anywhere hero for United.

But Stiles?—He was on the threshold of the Soccer scene.

United, of course, bought—and bought big—after Munich. Stan Crowther, Ernie Taylor, Albert Quixall . . . those were the quickfire signings. Then came Maurice Setters, Noel Cantwell, Pat Crerand, David Herd, Denis Law, John Connelly and Pat Dunne.

United poured hundreds of thousands of pounds into the transfer market, as they sought to recapture past glories and new honours. And Stiles was that most valued player of all—the admirable stand-in. But it isn't quite the same, somehow . . .

There were times when he lined up in attack; times when he played in the wing-half spot. But always, it seemed, there was someone who could more readily claim command of the position in the first team.

"I'll admit that I began to feel as though I were losing the battle to establish myself as a regular first-teamer with United," Nobby says candidly. "I'd have a few games, and then someone would come back after injury . . . and then I had to stand down again."

Nobby finally took the plunge and asked for a transfer. But United wouldn't let him go. At that time, I fancy, Nobby

||||||||||||||||||||||||||||||||||||||||

would have been content to join a Second Division club—just so long as he had the chance of a regular place in the first team.

With Maurice Setters dominating one wing-half position, it looked a pretty hopeless proposition, indeed, for Nobby Stiles when Pat Crerand arrived from Glasgow Celtic.

"There you had two players who, together, had cost the best part of £100,000 . . . so what chance had I? On the face of it, very little," says Nobby.

But, suddenly, the emphasis shifted. Suddenly, Maurice Setters moved to Stoke, and that last chance was Nobby's for the taking. He's never looked back.

"I don't think I ever lacked the confidence in my ability," he says. "But I had begun to feel it was an uphill fight trying to establish myself. When I got that chance, I was determined to snatch it. And look what's happened since!"

Stiles is now an automatic choice for the left-half position, and has established himself in the England team. He's certainly a hot tip to represent England in the World Cup—a far cry from those frustrating days of only a couple of years ago!

"Playing for England—and playing regularly in United's first-team line-up has helped me to mature," says Nobby. He still goes in hard—but he doesn't run into as much trouble as he used to do.

How hard he plays—and the knocks he takes—could be gauged by the bruises on a shin the day of the Rotherham-United Cup replay. And that was BEFORE the game.

How he's matured could be seen in the United-Benfica European Cup-tie at Old Trafford . . . when Nobby, of all people, surprised and delighted the fans by giving, schoolmaster style, a finger-wagging "wigging" to an opponent after a foul.

As I said, socially, he's a nice guy; on the field, he's a tiger. Just the sort of player England needs in the fight to win the World Cup for the first time. Can England do it? "I don't say we will—but I believe we CAN," says Nobby, firmly.

"We've bedded down into a pretty good team, all round. We have the right mixture of skill and fire, we have learned to blend with each other, and we can come back even after we're a goal down.

"More than anything, I want to play for England in the World Cup—and play for a victorious England team."

Like Alan Ball, his England buddy, Nobby Stiles hates to lose. And while England may yet make one or two changes in her final line-up, I believe Stiles will be still battling it out against the cream of the world's Soccer talent.

Nobby Stiles has won his personal battle for recognition; and, for my money, he can help England win the international battle for the Jules Rimet trophy. Good luck, Nobby—you deserve it!

DAVE CARTER

"Just sign it — we don't want your life story!"

▲ April 1964 | November 1966 ▶

To mark his being chosen as Footballer of the Year, Bobby Charlton was presented by Manchester United with a canteen of cutlery and a silver tea service. Here are manager Matt Busby and chairman Lewis Edwards making the club award.

The BEST that money can't buy

MILLIONS of words have been written about the dark-haired, Beatle-fringed youngster called George Best. Millions of words about his footballing skills, his with-it clothes, his fashion boutique just a few miles down the road from Old Trafford. And there will be millions more words written before George Best hangs up his boots.

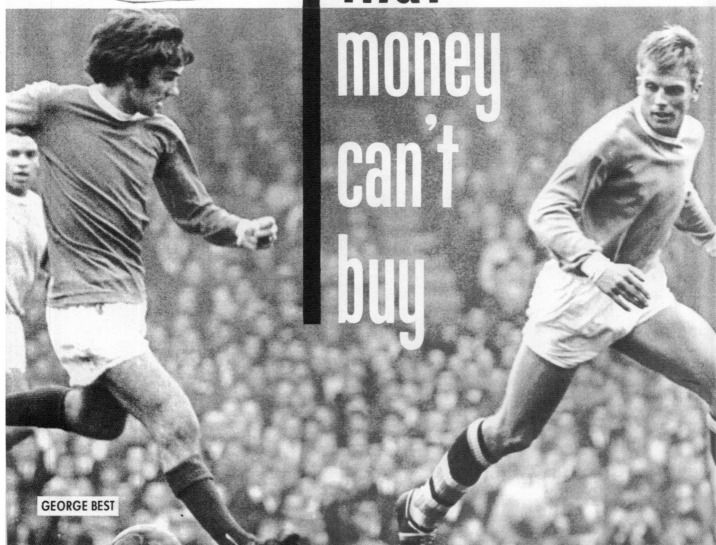

GEORGE BEST

▲ 1967–68 Gift Book

Whenever I think of this versatile, one-man band of Soccer entertainment, my mind goes back to two occasions . . . one at Old Trafford, one at the Partizan Soccer stadium in Belgrade. And both were important milestones in the life of George Best.

The first time, if memory serves me right, was at the end of December, 1963, when Manchester United had taken a real hammering from Burnley and there were some drastic changes in the United team for the Old Trafford return.

I had already been told by more than one Manchester United player that at Old Trafford they had an impish genius of a footballer from Ireland who before long would set the Soccer world on fire. Cautious through experience, I didn't argue — after all, I hadn't any proof that they were wrong. But I preferred to reserve judgment until I had seen for myself.

In that return against Burnley — a game in which United extracted ample revenge — I saw.

And as I watched the unknown boy Best making an impact, I remembered how Harry Gregg, then United's goalkeeper, had told me how this fellow-Irishman had "made a monkey" out of him during practice matches. At the end of those 90 minutes against Burnley, George Best had arrived. And Matt Busby had done it again — pulled an ace from his pack.

I was there, too, the day Manchester United went to Belgrade aiming to reach the final of the European Cup — and favourites that they were — to win it for the first time.

Partizan were United's opponents, and it was clear in those first, scoreless 45 minutes, that the Yugoslav team didn't really believe in their ability to beat the Red Devils from Old

Best carrying in supplies for his boutique.

Best besieged in his shop by young autograph-hunters.

Trafford. But in the second half, having realised that United had NOT sewn up the game, Partizan came out of their shell and scored two goals — enough to see them home by a 2-1 aggregate after the Old Trafford return.

I have discussed that game more than once since with Matt Busby, and plainly, like me, he believed victory was there for the taking by the United team. But on reflection, I am inclined to think that perhaps United lost that tie BEFORE they kicked the ball in earnest.

For George Best that day was playing with a bandage round a leg . . . and he was but a shadow of the player we have come to know.

The word "cartilage" was one which everybody seemed afraid even to whisper . . . but as Best limped on the plane for the homeward flight, it was plain that he would not play again until he had had this once-dreaded operation.

I pondered more than once . . . would Best be the same again, afterwards? And, no doubt, Matt Busby wondered . . . and hoped for the best.

Fortunately, George Best "came good" again after it was all over — even better, in fact, than he had been before. And as his fame grew, so did his fan club.

George Best, in fact, has become a Soccer institution — a pop idol to Soccer fans young and old. Less than three years ago, the George Best Fan Club numbered five — and three of them were the organisers! But see what's happened since. Now there are more than 1,000 members . . . with new ones enrolling every day.

In flow the letters — from all over Britain . . . and from places as far apart as France, Yugoslavia, Switzerland, Austria and Germany. Long before the end of last season, the fan mail was rolling in at the rate of almost 1,000 letters a week.

Which caused quite a prob-lem in itself. For it was found that to reply to all the letters would cost around £10 a week in stamps. There was only one answer — reply to those people who enclosed stamped, addressed envelopes.

Last Christmas, hundreds of cards arrived, too — one of them, painted by girls from Loughborough, was two feet square. One wall going up the stairs of the Best boutique was papered with fan mail.

Is Best worth all this hero-worship?—This quietly-spoken Irishman would probably beg leave to doubt it. But the fan mail and the fans are facts he cannot ignore . . . and, of course, they are as welcome as the flowers in May. For so long as they flourish, so does George Best.

Certainly, Best has made an impact upon Soccer. In his short spell at Old Trafford he has become a first-team fixture and an automatic choice for Northern Ireland. And to think that at the start of it all he went back to the old country because he was homesick!

Today, if I were a manager and being given my pick of Bobby Charlton, Denis Law or George Best, I would take the Irish boy.

I have seen Law take a game by the scruff of the neck and make it go Manchester United's way; I have seen Charlton come as near to Soccer perfection as is possible. But I would still take Best. Whenever he gets the ball, I feel a stir of anticipation, of excitement . . . because as well as being a footballing thoroughbred, he is an entertainer.

Over the years, Matt Busby has earned a reputation as a manager not afraid to go out and speculate heavily in the transfer market, especially when seeking the best players money could buy.

Today, whatever transfer ventures Busby may make, he has on his Old Trafford books a genuine star who cost him nothing. The Best, in fact, that money CAN'T buy . . .

▲ January 1967

THE CHAMPIONS.

MANCHESTER UNITED

Back row: Sadler, Crerand, Stiles, Stepney, No

▲ November 1967

HERD . . . played 28 League games before injury.

es. Front row: Aston, Charlton, Law, Best, Dunne.

BRENNAN . . . made 16 League appearances.

FOOTBALLER OF THE YEAR

THE BEST SECRET IS OUT

The George Best Matchmaker by Stylo designed after many months' research and testing and already acclaimed as a major breakthrough by leading players and managers alike.

Good looks team with first-class design to make this the Soccer Shoe of the century – the BEST ! As comfortable as slippers, as strong as climbing boots – yet as light and streamlined as a track shoe.

Builds confidence, improves the game.

THE MOST REVOLUTIONARY SOCCER SHOE EVER

GEORGE BEST STYLO Matchmakers

GO FOR THE BEST

1. Best comfort
2. Best ball control. Perfectly smooth vamp. No lacing where the ball is kicked.
3. Interchangeable and Multi-stud models.
4. Triple-tone leather uppers, Black, Burgundy and White.
5. Revolutionary side lacing. Field and laboratory tests prove beyond doubt that this shoe gives 25% more support where needed.
6. Special sole designed for greater flexibility, lightness and wear.
* Made on a brand new exclusive last with low line toeshape. Boys 65/11 Mens 95/11 to 147/-

BEST FITTING · BEST COMFORT · BEST BALL CONTROL

A PRODUCT OF THE STYLO-BARRATT SPORTS DIVISION CONWAY ROAD LEEDS 8
SEE THEM, TRY THEM ON AT YOUR SPORTS SHOP NOW

▲ August 1968 | May 1968 ▶

MATT BUSBY
Man & Manager

A SPECIAL "FOOTBALL MONTHLY" PROFILE

MATT BUSBY — MAN an

Football Monthly's
team of
specialist writers,
in these pages
tell the story of
one of the most
remarkable men
in world football

I T began in a two-roomed miner's cottage in the little Lanark-shire hamlet of Orbiston, close by Motherwell. It will reach its climax only when, with handkerchief hurried out to mop away the effort and emotion of watching the accomplishment, he savours the sight of Manchester United team with the European Cup.

For without this official seal on his beloved United as the greatest club side in Europe, the Matt Busby story will never be as complete as he would want it.

It is neither pot-hunting—Nor seeking for self-glory which lights this fierce ambition in the man. It is pride for a club, prestige for our game and just sheer professionalism.

To know the man is to know these fundamental truths.

Bestriding the ferocious competition that is today's game as un-questionably the greatest manager there has been would breed an understandable self-satisfaction in many people.

But with Matt Busby this is related into terms of pride and ambition *only for the club he has served for nearly 23 years.* As, indeed, are the personal honours of a C.B.E. and the freedom of Manchester, recently accorded to him.

Thirty-eight years spent in Manchester and Liverpool have long since transplanted his roots and affections from Lanarkshire to Lancashire.

"Manchester has been good to me—it's my home. I wouldn't want to live anywhere else," he will tell you.

But, as a dutiful son, he still turns his footsteps homewards, when he can, to the background which formed the character and forged the strength of personality which has been tested at the heights and the depths.

He wrote in his book, "My Story" . . .

"So many of the good things in life have come my way since I became a professional footballer, it sometimes does me good to think back on the days when living was not so easy. It helps to keep my feet on the ground . . ."

That "not so easy" is a typically quiet understatement. In harsh fact the sniper's bullet in the First World War which killed his father, left a family of three girls and Matt, at six-years-of-age the eldest child, for Mrs. Busby to fend for.

And out of those hard days when he saw his mother scurry around to see to her little family before going off to a job at the pit-top . . . of the search for other work to support them when depression came to the coalmines . . . was imparted the humility of the really big man, the sympathetic understanding of one who has looked trial and tribulation square in the face.

And helped him keep his feet on the ground.

Matt Busby, with his slowly widening smile, his air of fullest attention to even the most trivial remark, and head lowered to catch every detail, like a priest in the confessional, has shared the confid-ences of the eminent. Courteously borne, the plaints of the ordinary; his natural-art is to make the latter seem equally important of a hearing.

In a business often petty and peevish, often unbalanced with its brush-stroke speed from success to failure, he has long since won regard and respect. Won them in the fullest measure without once courting them.

He can make a raw, small team-manager, feel that his trials and hopes have parity with those of United and Old Trafford.

This writer saw it happen, as a travel-ling companion of Matt on a long journey, sequel to a match in which United had just lost a star defender through injury and with a big Cup game as United's next match.

Further down the train was an earnest new manager of a small Third Division club. When he heard he was there, and never having met him, Matt Busby asked me to see if he would join us.

Then, with his own worry seemingly set aside, he sat and listened to plans, hopes —and fears—as just another manager with the self-same trials.

Matt Busby never knew how much that meeting meant to a manager now established in his own right. I do. His sincere understanding and attention won another Busby admirer that day.

He is a fine after-dinner speaker with a goodly helping of his native wit. He loves a good story—particularly a football one —like the next.

He says: "Every manager should have a hobby. Mine is Soccer!" And he means just that.

For the only time he ever gets away from it is when he plays a round of golf. He likes to read, but seldom gets time. Even the social round inevitably turns to football—and United.

The Busby family comprises Mrs. Jea Busby, daughter Sheena and Matt's son Alex, better known as "Sandy". Jea Busby is the one who takes the edge of the day, the sting out of defeat for he husband . . . and Matt is the first to admi it.

But Sheena, through her marriage t Don Gibson, forced Matt to sell a playe he wanted to keep; the circumstances als showed how quick and decisive he can b when action is called for.

His daughter began to go out wit Gibson, a wing-half who joined Unite from school. Then the couple becam engaged . . . and Matt had a problem How could a prospective son-in-law g along at Old Trafford while the manage his future father-in-law, tried to treat hi as just another player?

The answer came quickly. In a matc following the announcement of the engagement Don Gibson was not havin a happy time. And a terrace critic said h piece with a few well-chosen word There and then Matt Busby made up h mind that the situation was not good fc club, player or manager. Gibson wa transferred to Sheffield Wednesday.

Matt Busby didn't allow a simila repeat when "Sandy" began to sho promise. The younger Busby played som games for Bury, for amateurs Kingstonia

THIS IS OUR SPECIAL TRIBUTE

MANAGER

and later for Blackburn because ex-United skipper Johnny Carey was Rovers' manager at the time.

The courage of Matt Busby in making big decisions was shown in the making-up and breaking-up of United teams when he saw his high standards not quite being met.

But cruel fate caused the break-up of what many consider would have been the greatest team British football had seen . . . the snow and sleet of Munich in February, 1958 did that in one of Soccer's greatest tragedies.

The story has long since been told of how a team died that day, of the journalists who died with them.

Only those closest to him will ever know how he survived and came back to start the job of putting United back on top all over again.

For apart from his own injuries, his long and lonely fight in an oxygen tent to will himself back to life, there was the burden—as he has always carried it—of feeling for the brilliant youngsters he fathers through to stardom.

He has taken on all their disappointments when the big prize has been missed. He has been their confidant in worried times on and off the field just as much as he has shared their great success. *Munich left its mark for a long time physically. It still does mentally.*

No-one earns such world-wide respect for courtesy and charm alone. But there is steel in the man, as several great players well know. They know that when they let him down they will be told of it. When they let United down, more forcibly so.

The demand to stay on after a training session—"the boss wants to say a few words"—can mean an uncomfortable wait for the brightest stars at Old Trafford.

There, with the door closed firmly after him, Matt Busby can read the riot act out with the firmest disciplinarian.

When Denis Law made demands before re-signing for the 1966-67 season, and a transfer if they were not met, he got a quick answer . . . a place on the transfer list.

Said Busby, "Only one person tells me what to do—my wife, Jean."

And he followed up: "No one issues an ultimatum to Manchester United." Happily for club and player peace was restored.

Recently when stories were sparked off about his possible retirement he turned them aside as a joke.

"I'll retire when I feel I have nothing to offer to the game . . . and I hope that won't be for a long time," he countered.

A HOPE WE ALL FERVENTLY SHARE.

Matt Busby proudly showing his C.B.E. to his wife, Jean, and son "Sandy" outside Buckingham Palace. Below, he receives the Freedom of Manchester from the Lord Mayor, Alderman Mrs. Elizabeth Yarwood, J.P.

MATT BUSBY

Man and Manager

IT is surely a measure of Matt Busby's unique managerial ability to pick the right type of player that of the very first successful side he built up in his early days with Manchester United, no fewer than five players themselves became managers.

They were Johnny Carey, Allenby Chilton, Jack Rowley, Stan Pearson and Charlie Mitten. Two more stalwarts of that still-remembered 1948 F.A. Cup-winning team—one of the finest Busby ever made—Jack Crompton and Johnny Aston, are still with Matt as head trainer and chief coach respectively.

Of Busby's own pre-war playing contemporaries, Cliff Britton, Stanley Cullis and Joe Mercer, a one-time outstanding England half-back line, are still managing English League clubs; so too, is Archie Macaulay, a colleague in Scotland's team for Busby's last war-time international.

None, of course, can match Busby's long service as a manager which is approached by only one other, Bert Tann of Bristol Rovers, who has handed over the reins at Eastville to a younger man after 21 years.

Picking the right men . . . that has been the bed rock of Busby's success. The uncanny knack of buying the right men at the right time . . . of delegating

JIMMY MURPHY . . . Busby's right-hand man.

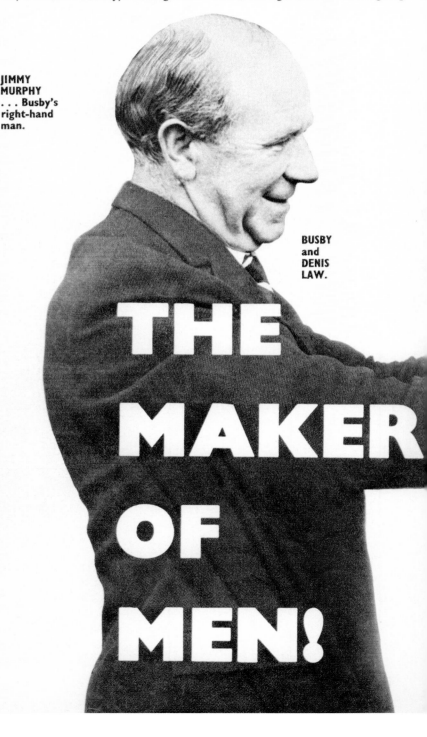

BUSBY and DENIS LAW.

THE MAKER OF MEN!

responsibility to the right men—like Jimmy Murphy, Joe Armstrong and Jack Crompton and John Aston, for instance.

That . . . and the carefully organised recruiting system which has ensured an unending flow of talented youngsters under the Old Trafford umbrella for the 22 momentous years that Busby has been the boss.

But he has always been prepared to spend heavily to get the men he wanted—when there happened not to be a youngster on hand to do the job!

Years ago Busby was determined to get Johnny Berry from Birmingham. It took him nearly two seasons but in the end he was quite prepared to cough up £25,000—a large sum then—for a man who was to pay it back tenfold before Munich ended his career.

When Busby wanted Denis Law he did not think twice about paying a then record £116,000 to Turin. The labourer was worth his hire . . .

Unlike that other prolific spender, Bill Nicholson of Spurs, who has bought, rather than made a team, Busby has banked on his unique youth assembly line on which to fashion United's unparalleled post-war success.

Of his current side, only Alex Stepney, David Herd, Tony Dunne and Pat Crerand cost fees, apart from Law. The remainder—even the brilliantly talented George Best—have all been groomed for stardom—the most efficient grooming in the business, judged by results.

This was what Busby had in mind when he became Manchester United's manager in October, 1945. Then, Old Trafford was a blitzed wreck and his club were struggling under the burden of a £15,000 overdraft.

And as soon as he had put together the nucleus of that splendid side which won the Cup in 1948, Busby set in motion his youth policy—the end product of which was to become worth a fortune to the club—the Busby Babes.

Literally, hundreds of highly talented young footballers passed through Old Trafford in the years which followed. Some never quite made the grade, others enjoyed only fleeting success but as many again developed into internationals.

Busby has never hesitated to draft these fledglings into his League side when he considered the time was ripe. This season alone, there have been several such occasions—hence the emergence of Brian Kidd, Jimmy Ryan, John Fitzpatrick and others.

It is this brand of managerial astuteness which makes all the difference between prolonged and only temporary success. Busby has always been looking twelve months ahead and because of his foresight his club remain the envy of most of the others in the Football League.

Many have followed Busby's post-war youth pattern but only a few—Everton and Leeds among them—anything like as successfully.

It is believed that United employ fewer scouts than other First Division clubs of similar standing. But results suggest that the Old Trafford set-up is twice as effective!

Busby's other great forté has been his shrewdness in switching a player's position—often with devastating effect.

This stems from his own experiences as a young player with Manchester City. While struggling to make the grade—and struggling hard, according to his own story—he found no success until moved from inside-forward to right-half—where he spent the remainder of his playing career.

In his first season at Old Trafford,

LAW . . . at £116,000, worth his hire.

JACK ROWLEY . . . became a manager —one of five.

Busby conducted a series of positional permutations which provided the key to his initial successes.

He realised that his two inside-men Johnny Carey and John Aston would make better full-backs; that Allenby Chilton would be more effective as a centre-half than a wing-half. All three became internationals and Carey and Aston could play anywhere.

Talking of Busby's "hunches" . . . it was about this time that he paid a mere £4,000 for Jimmy "brittle bones" Delaney —a veteran suspected to be injury-prone. Matt got six magnificent years out of the old Celtic star, then sold him to Aberdeen at only £500 less than he cost.

It is rare for a manager to have taken such a calculated risk at such a crucial time and seen it pay such handsome dividends. At least one, in recent seasons, paid £100,000 for a complete misfit!

It all seems long ago but it was in this teething period that Busby laid the foundation stone of his stature as the greatest manager since the hey-day of Herbert Chapman and Major Frank Buckley.

The years have fled by and Manchester United's repute has become world-wide while we have marvelled at the successive teams which Busby has built up, broken up, then re-built again off a blueprint of acumen, patience, money and inspiration.

Meantime rivals have waited for a decline and fall which still seems as unlikely as it was a decade ago—before Munich.

Munich (1958) destroyed what many believe would have been the greatest of all United sides . . . destroyed a wealth of youth and skill . . . Edwards, Taylor, Pegg, Jones, Byrne . . . Whelan . . . Colman . . . among others.

It almost destroyed Busby, too, but eventually he was ready to build yet again on the tremendous salvage job done in the interim by Jimmy Murphy.

Since that tragedy United have won two more League championships and another F.A. Cup victory to add to the brilliant title wins of 1951-52, 1955-56

ROGER BYRNE (above) and DUNCAN EDWARDS (below) . . . part of Busby's great wealth of talent.

and 1956-57 and the earlier Cup success of 1948.

Only Wolves, between 1953 and 1959, can in any way match this, with three League championships and a Cup win. And remember, in Busby's time, United have six times finished runners-up in the First Division—three times in successive seasons ('47, '48 and '49) and twice runners-up at Wembley.

Wolves, too, were thrice runners-up in the title race. But Cullis has long left the scene of his Molineux glories. *Busby is still the master of Old Trafford.*

The United triumphs have been achieved by successive sides of youth and experience — or rather, steadily

improving youth blended with youthful experience.

The average age of United's first team has lowered recently following the departures of Noel Cantwell, Maurice Setters and Harry Gregg. Only Bill Foulkes, of the immediate post-Munich staff, survives as a first teamer.

Munich apart — and Busby hardly speaks of it now—his greatest disappointment has been his failure so far to win the coveted European Cup.

He has striven for it constantly since he first led United into Europe in season 1956-57 in the face of Football League "warnings" about fixture congestion.

Busby realised long ago the hard cash to be had out of the lucrative European inter-club competitions.

Long ago, Busby was attracted by the challenge Europe offered. He needed to match his young side against the best on the continent. On the horizon was a glittering trophy, possession of which would set the seal on a dozen years of high achievement.

As this is written, Matt Busby and United still await that elusive prize. A fellow Scot—Jock Stein—has won it for Celtic but no English club has yet taken the most sought-after trophy, outside the World Cup.

Since 1957, United have reached the semi-finals of the competition each time they qualified:- 1956-57—beaten by Real Madrid; 1957-58—beaten by A.C. Milan (after Munich); 1965-66—beaten by Partizan Belgrade; 1967-68—v. Real again.

In 1958-59 they were invited to compete by way of tribute to their past services to European football but were prevented from doing so by the Football League on the grounds that they were not national champions.

Of the other British clubs who have played in the European Cup: Hibernian (1956), Rangers (1960), Spurs (1962), Dundee (1963) and Liverpool (1965) have each reached the semi-final once, with Celtic achieving ultimate success last year. Otherwise, Manchester United's record has been by far the best.

Busby means to win the European Cup. The question is . . . will it be this year or when? The matter of first winning the First Division championship would seem to be incidental, as far as this last burning ambition is concerned.

The elder statesman among our managers is now 57. He has 22 years of United triumphs and troubles behind him and there can be only a mite he does not know about the game, scarcely an emotion he has not experienced.

He has been wise before his time. In 1957, for instance, he was advocating the abolition of the maximum wage limit, shortening of the League fixture list and smaller and less expensive playing staffs for hard-up clubs, among other innovations.

Chapman . . . Buckley . . . Busby. They have been the giants among our managers of the modern football age. Maybe it will be Busby who will stand on his own in the fullness of time. Already, at Old Trafford, his place is almost that of an immortal.

MATT BUSBY—Man and Manager

HOW OTHERS SEE HIM...

DENIS LAW

JOE MERCER

ARTHUR ROWE

BOBBY CHARLTON

"TO GIVE advice or criticism requires diplomacy of a high order. Matt Busby manages it somehow. I have even known him get away with the impossible one—telling a player he is not trying hard enough! If there is an accusation to make a player bridle it is that one. With most managers it would mean a transfer request or a first-class row.

"But not with the Boss. He takes his man aside and talks to him quietly: 'you are not trying hard enough. You must give that much more'.

"The reaction is odd. No tantrums, no protestations. A toughened professional will almost certainly feel that he has got to put more into it because he is letting down two people—himself and the Boss.

"Basis of this feeling, which I take to be rare, is the fact that we, the players, know that he gives everything to United without going on the field. He gives his intelligence, his knowledge, his energy, his charm, his integrity, his courage. We feel it is our job to repay him".
BOBBY CHARLTON (*"My Soccer Life"*)

●

"THE STORIES about him are legion. There are people who say he is too remote, and that he does not control the players, and exercise sufficient discipline. Some say that he is too content to let the team play football by ear, instead of concentrating on tactics, in an era notable for tactics that are strangling the game as an entertainment.

"All this is eyewash, of course. Mr. Busby is a diplomat. He accomplishes his aims quietly, if possible without fuss, but with an iron determination.

"Some critics accuse him of being too tolerant of rough players on his staff, but I can assure them that he has, through the years, weeded out any players he has considered to come into the category of 'dirty'.

"Anyone who does not toe the line at Old Trafford can get away with it for a time but eventually, the Boss will drop on him like a ton of bricks."
BILL FOULKES (*"Back at the Top"*).

●

"MATT was one of the most entertaining and cultured players of his day. He has proved himself to be the outstanding manager of his time.

"But to those of us who know him intimately, the most striking characteristic about the man is that one could not wish to meet a nicer fellow".
CLIFF BRITTON (*Manager, Hull City*).

●

"I'VE KNOWN Matt Busby as a great name, and as a counsellor who has helped and advised me, since I was only a kid of sixteen. Nothing that has happened since has lessened my respect for him. Quite the contrary.

"People ask me why he is such a great manager, and it is hard to put one's finger on the precise reason. Perhaps he has got something that the others lack—I'll call it 'human approach'. He is not only worried about the team winning but that the individual players should do well for themselves.

"Mr. Busby shows a real interest in all his teams. It is the League side which is his bread-and-butter, but he will go out of his way to explain to a boy why he has been left out of the sixth team.

"He knows how hurt a lad could be by failing to find his name listed on the notice board. Though tough enough to make a bold decision when it's required, Matt Busby always tries to soften the blow for anyone concerned.

"Another important thing is that our boss has been through the mill himself to become a distinguished internationalist."
DENIS LAW (*"Living for Kicks"*).

"QUITE SIMPLY—Matt is a good fellow. A person of whom one is very pleased to be able to say 'yes I know him well'. A man who has achieved greatness on and off the field with his good head and big heart".
ARTHUR ROWE (*Assistant-Manager, Crystal Palace*).

●

"MATT BUSBY is without a shadow of a doubt, I suppose, Mister Football. He is the first person most fans think of when they think of football managers. And as far as players are concerned, well, he's a kind of idol . . .

"He has also built his own image into something approaching a legend in the game. All this is due to his shrewd attitude to the game and its players—and also very largely to his qualities as a man".
NOEL CANTWELL (*Manager, Coventry City*).

●

"SOME OF US are happy to produce one good side—Matt has produced four and perhaps there is a fifth one coming through. Matt is certainly the best manager of good players I know. A player stands or falls in his eyes on his ability alone. Other things aren't so important. He can charm people into playing or even thinking his way. But when the occasion warrants it he can be ruthless in the interests of Manchester United.

"Once a player has outlived his usefulness at Old Trafford 'his feet never touch'. The success he has had hasn't affected him—but the success he hasn't had has left a mark. He badly wants to win the European Cup, not for himself but for Manchester United. Personally, I think he deserves it himself".
JOE MERCER
(*Manager, Manchester City*).

BILLY FOULKES

NOEL CANTWELL

CLIFF BRITTON

Top: Chelsea defenders Harris, Boyle and Thomson move in as George Best gains control. Below: Tony Dunne manages to clear fro

▲ June 1968

THE SPIRIT OF THE UNITED!

Recording a rare happening at Old Trafford . . . Manchester United fighting a losing battle against Chelsea. It comes to all great teams at some time, even to United.

But again this season United have fought the good Soccer fight, and with success. The crowds following them have been greater than those on any other ground. The quality of their football has been as high as ever, the skill, the flair and the personalities in their ranks continue to bring them world-wide acclaim.

From manager Matt Busby the creed is inherited—that only the best is good enough at Old Trafford.

THAT IS THE SPIRIT OF THE UNITED.

Below: The ball finished in the net after Brian Kidd's acrobatic effort—Chelsea's Webb does a hand-stand.

The night a nation sat and watched . . .

BUSBY'S NIGHT!

ON a lovely, sun-drenched May evening, with the roads and side streets of England deserted and quiet as a nation moved into the sitting-room to become part of a 200-million TV audience across the world, a man and his team realised their dream when Manchester United became European Cup-holders.

It was not a night or a game for the academic or the analytical. It was a night of high emotion and heart and eventually tears.

It was a night, too, of unashamed bias.

For more than two hours nothing else mattered but that Matt Busby and Bobby Charlton, Stiles, Best, Stepney, Foulkes and the rest should take that Cup to Manchester and England for the first time.

It was a night that was to

▲ 1968–69 Gift Book

Arms raised in triumph, Brian Kidd, nineteen-years-old on the day, salutes the header by Bobby Charlton (centre) which put United in the lead. Keeper Henrique can only stand and stare.

end a 12-year-quest for Busby, Charlton and Foulkes, survivors of the Munich plane crash which cruelly destroyed another United side chasing that same dream.

Benfica, champions of Portugal, twice previous winners of the trophy, and the last barrier to Busby's greatest ambition, were there only to make the number up so far as more than 90,000 Wembley watchers and the overwhelming majority of that vast TV audience were concerned.

It was World Cup time again here at home.

The morning and evening rush hours on the Tube and the buses, the hours up to the kick-off had no other conversation except,

temporarily for the Derby, run in the afternoon.

Which was as quickly forgotten!

In the end it was a fantastic evening—which could only happen to Matt Busby and his often wayward United. It could have been a script written by himself.

Go back over that evening . . .

The chances United missed, which should have seen them easy winners long before the end . . . Bobby Charlton getting his first European Cup goal for two years . . . United losing their lead for hopes to sink . . . Stepney's magnificent save from Eusebio when all seemed lost . . .

Then the agonies of extra time with Busby, going among his so

Pat Crerand lies motionless after a clash with Eusebio as players of both teams get steamed up about it.

The gap-tooth grin again . . . you saw it in the World Cup, here it is again—Nobby Stiles (left) and Bobby Charlton and Billy Foulkes. Below, the men who did so much. There's Alex Stepney (left) and Charlton (again) with the trophy.

tired players, calling for a last great effort . . . and the answer, three wonderful goals in eight minutes. Finally, a shattered Benfica and United composedly playing out time.

Stiles beating the turf . . . Charlton turning a somersault . . . Eusebio going round to each rival with congratulations . . . his players trying to drag Busby up to the presentation, and the long, deep and emotional walk back to the dressing room by Matt with the cheers growing louder with his every step.

Gone then was all thought of the mediocrity of the first half . . . and the mean and frequent fouls . . . the too rigid refereeing threatening to ruin a game which eventually lived up to its promise.

ON SECOND THOUGHTS MATT BUSBY HIMSELF WOULDN'T HAVE DARED TO WRITE WHAT WE SAW THAT STUPENDOUS EVENING LAST MAY.

If I live to be 100 I shall never forget my 19th birthday

by
BRIAN KIDD
Manchester United

WHAT a birthday present! Football has been my life for as long as I can remember, and certainly from the tender age of eight when I first played for my school.

During the following three years I became so obsessed with the game that I even skipped my 11-plus—just so that I could leave school at fifteen. For a year previously I had signed on schoolboy forms for Manchester United.

From the moment I became a full-time member of the United pool of players, my life and career seemed to reach one pinnacle after another.

My first game with the reserves (I signed professional forms at 17) . . . being chosen as substitute for the League side . . . my League debut . . . my first goal for the first team—all were great moments.

But no matter what I have so far achieved, or what may be in store, I don't think anything can match the thrill, the excitement, the overpowering feeling of achievement that my 19th birthday gave me.

It was Wednesday, May 29, 1968, also the date of United's great triumph against Benfica at Wembley in the final of the European Cup!

And I was the lucky one to score the third goal for the Reds—the one that put the issue beyond doubt.

If I live to be a hundred, I shall never forget the sight of the ball hitting the back of the net from my header. Not only do I still dream about it—even in my waking hours I still see the incident as though it had happened only minutes previously.

My chance came as Bobby Charlton headed into the six yard box, I headed it goalwards, goalkeeper Henrique could only palm the ball out, back it came to me—and over his head it went into the net. *What a birthday present!*

That was certainly *my* great moment, just as our victory was for the Boss and for the team. What a lucky guy I am to have been part of this great club success—and in my first season, too!

Mind you, I also had one of my worst moments in that match—and that goes for most of the team. It was when, shortly before the end of 90 minutes, with the score 1-1, we saw that goal-scorer supreme, Eusebio, going through at full speed.

My heart sank, but up came that hero, Alex Stepney, to make a brilliant save which gave us the extra time in which to clinch the victory that had eluded the club for so many long years.

The glamour of that night at Wembley seemed a far cry from my schoolboy days at St. Patrick's School, in Collyhurst, Manchester. I played for the school's fourth team at the earliest possible age (8) and progressed through to the first team and played a full season for Manchester Boys in the side that won the Manchester County Schools Cup.

It was while playing for Manchester Boys that I was spotted by United's famous scout, Mr. Joe Armstrong, who first took me to Old Trafford.

And here I must pay tribute to three people who helped me a lot in those formative years, my school-teachers Mr. James Goggins, Mr. Laurie Cassidy and Mr. John Mulligan—particularly the former who gave me good advice when it came to signing schoolboy forms.

After leaving school, I played a full season in United's "B" team, and at sixteen I became a regular member of the Central League side. At 17 I was chosen as substitute for a League game v. Fulham, but wasn't called upon to play.

Then, in the summer of 1967 I was a member of the United party chosen to tour America, Australia and New Zealand and played in several games as players were switched around.

Then came the opening game of the 1967-68 season, the Charity Shield final at Old Trafford v. Spurs. As David Herd was still out of action with a broken leg, I knew I had a chance. Sure enough, I was chosen for my debut on home soil.

And believe it or not, Mr. Goggins, who was on holiday in Bournemouth, drove the 220 miles to Manchester to see me play—and drove back again after the game to complete his holiday.

With that kind of loyalty and support I just *had* to grab my big chance with both hands. I was lucky, for I was able to hold my place throughout the season, scoring 15 league goals and two in the European Cup—including that fantastic final!

As for the future . . . well, we at Old Trafford (and I'm proud to be able to say "we") have two targets to aim for this new season—to retain the European Cup, and to regain the First Division Championship from our rivals across the town, Manchester City.

This may be aiming high, but we shall strain every nerve and sinew to achieve it. Wish us luck . . .

It's there, in the circle, put there by Kidd against Benfica.

▲ September 1968

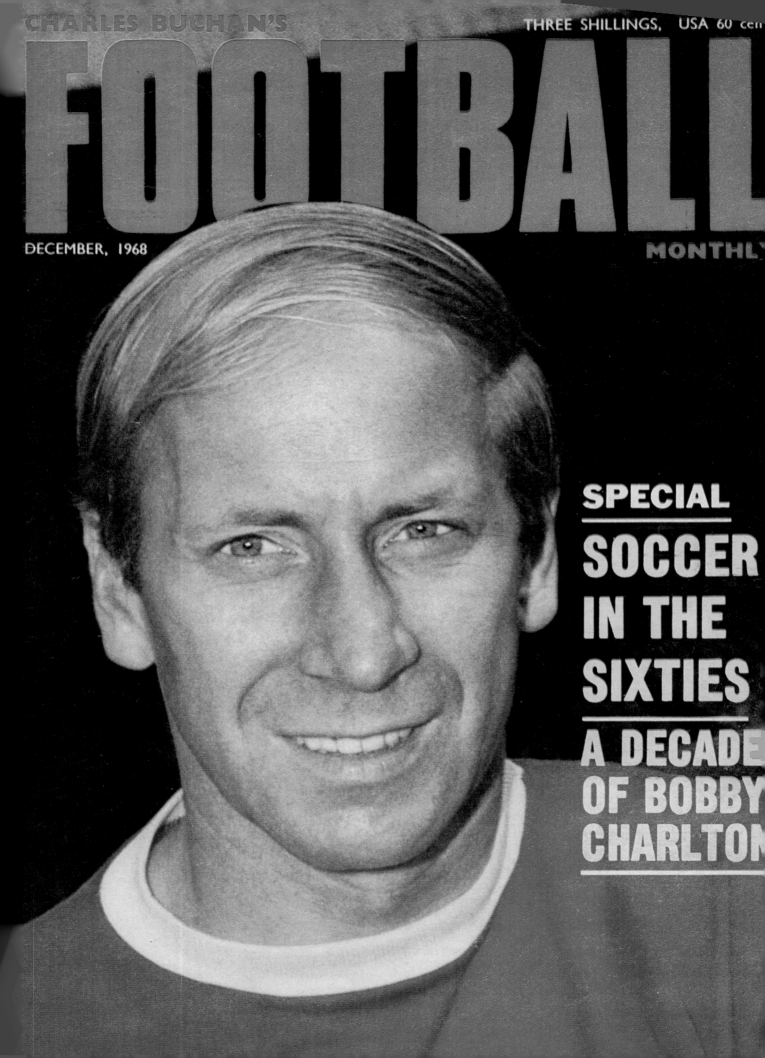

CHARLES BUCHAN'S

FOOTBALL

THREE SHILLINGS, USA 60 cen

DECEMBER, 1968

MONTHLY

SPECIAL

SOCCER IN THE SIXTIES

A DECADE OF BOBBY CHARLTON

SIR MATT
moves upstairs

It had to come. Fortunately, it won't be a complete break when Sir Matt Busby leaves the Old Trafford dressing-rooms and the playing pitch to his successor as Manchester United's manager at the end of the season—he steps up to become the new general manager. Twenty-three years under Busby have been filled with magic moments for United. Tragic moments, too. His record shows two FA Cup victories, five League titles and present possession of the European Cup. His legacy is that of the man who has made the greatest single contribution to the game in his time. Here are some of the highlights of his career . . .

(1) July, 1968 . . . and now it is SIR Matt Busby; (2) May, 1963 . . . United have beaten Leicester in the FA Cup Final; (3) May, 1968: With Jimmy Murphy spreading quiet encouragement before extra time which won the European Cup; (4) And there's that Cup, now United's, as Busby had vowed it would be.

▲ March 1969

▲ April 1969

NOBBY STILES — is there, was there, another like him?

SINCE the World Cup of 1966, Nobby Stiles, of Manchester United and England, has had to live with a reputation for being a relentlessly hard player. It's a reputation which has brought him cat-calls and piercing whistles on the Continent. And one with which he now has to live.

This season, crowds in Britain have not been slow to jump on the band-wagon of the boo-boys, and the question is: IS Nobby getting TOO much stick from the fans? I have heard him subjected to barracking even BEFORE he has kicked the ball. . . .

For a player who goes in hard it is inevitable that at times he misses the ball and it is the opponent who suffers. For soccer is a game of physical contact. And not every tackle can be timed perfectly.

When it comes to booing a footballer before he has even gone near an opponent, though, it makes me wonder if Nobby Stiles is being made to suffer too much.

What do Nobby's Old Trafford team-mates think? Wing-half Pat Crerand has no doubts about one thing: "This is something that Nobby will have to accept. But I'm sure that Nobby doesn't bother about it.

"On the Continent it is really noticeable, of course. The fans there give him some stick the moment Nobby goes near an opponent.

"Many players on the Continent regard themselves as almost sacrosanct, they will think nothing of shirt-tugging and obstruction, even committing a physical foul. But they DON'T relish close marking and keen tackling."

Paddy Crerand adds: "The way Nobby plays is a part of his make-up, and the crowd gets at him, with his reputation. One accidental foul . . . and that's it."

United goalkeeper Alex Stepney thinks Nobby is being treated a little unfairly even by British fans who are used to seeing plenty of hard tackling and physical contact. "In some of our away games this season," said Alex, "the first time Nobby has gone for the ball—even if it's been running loose—some characters on the terraces have started to boo.

"That's not on, really. Supporters are entitled to express their opinions, whether it's by booing or cheering, but at least they should wait until a player has done something to deserve cat-calls before opening up.

"When England won the World Cup, Nobby was a hero—and rightly. Now some folk seem to have gone to the other extreme. They're out to make Nobby a villain the moment he runs on the field.

"And I've noticed that they don't go out of their way to applaud when—as happens quite often—he sportingly picks the ball up and hands it to an opponent or the referee when a free-kick has been awarded against United."

For good measure, here is the view of a player who is NOT one of Nobby's club-mates . . . Everton and England forward Alan Ball. He has played alongside Nobby Stiles in the England team, and against him in the League.

Alan says: "I think it is a case of a player having had a reputation thrust on him . . . and once you have been tagged with a reputation for being a hard player it stays." Alan agrees that some fans nowadays seem to be ready to jump on Nobby's back. But, like Paddy Crerand, he says: "I don't think he lets it bother him."

Alan added :"Nobby is a true professional. He goes out to do a job to the best of his ability, and no matter what the supporters of opposing teams may say, he does that job very efficiently."

Nobby Stiles may be out of favour with some football supporters; they may even take him to task unfairly, at times. But it could be that beneath it all there lurks respect and fear—fear that he will prove an effective stumbling block to their hopes of victory for their own team.

PAT CRERAND . . . "Nobby doesn't bother" ▼

THE SUPPLIER

JOE ARMSTRONG, 75-yr-old ace-scout who lands the stars at Old Trafford, talks about his job to JERRY DAWSON

GEOFF Whitefoot, Denis Viollet, Don Gibson, Wilf McGuinness, Mark Jones, Bobby Charlton, Steve James, Nobby Stiles, Brian Kidd . . . this is not an attempt to name a dream side of Manchester United stars past and present.

It is merely a list of *some* of the players who arrived at Old Trafford under the wing of a sprightly 75-year-old who appears to have discovered the elixir of eternal youth, JOE ARMSTRONG!

It is he who provides the steady supply of "Busby Babes" for the Old Trafford production line. He it is who quietly and without any ballyhoo, spends hours, days even, watching schoolboy players, assessing their skill and potential, and persuading the boys and their parents that their future in Soccer lies at Old Trafford.

But he steadfastly claims that he does *not* "discover" them, and doesn't like the word to be applied to his work. This is his story:

Discovery is not the right word. It is usually a boy's schoolmaster, watching him over a long period, knowing his background and temperament, who first recognises his ability —and tips-off a club.

At Manchester United we have only eight scouts. Without tips from outside interested parties, we certainly wouldn't be physically able to see all the players who eventually find a niche on our playing staff. We would be bound to miss a lot of them!

For example, I am credited with having discovered Duncan Edwards and Bobby Charlton. I was responsible for finally bringing Charlton to Old Trafford all right, but in Duncan's case, he was first recommended to us by Reg Preece, a part-time scout, in his home town of Dudley, Worcs. (a moulder by trade) and it was the late Bert Whalley who signed him. But without Reg we would probably never have heard of him!

By the same rule, we would probably have missed Bobby Charlton, had we not been tipped-off by the headmaster of his school. These are the original discoverers of most players, and it is a pity that they rarely receive the credit due to them.

There is a lot of luck in the scouting game, too, in fact, I would put it as high as 60 per cent! I remember one occasion when I went to Cardiff to watch a young player, and sitting next to me in the stand was a party of four, obviously, mother, father, grandma and grandad, of one of the boys.

They *were* the parents and grand-parents

▲ July 1969

OF **TALENT**

of the boy *I was watching*. I was able to talk to them during the interval and after the game—and I got the lad!

As recently as last year, I went to watch a boy in the England v. Scotland Schoolboy International at White Hart Lane, and I saw a lady inadvertently drop an envelope. I picked it up, gave it back to her, and we got into conversation.

I quickly found out that she was the mother of the player who interested me—and the boy is now one of our youth players at Old Trafford!

Dealing with parents is an important part of my work—and, here I will let you into a little secret. When I am trying to convince dubious parents that their son's future lies in Soccer in general, and at Old Trafford in particular, I pay most attention to the mother!

Don't get me wrong, I don't try to kid her along, for I believe in being honest at

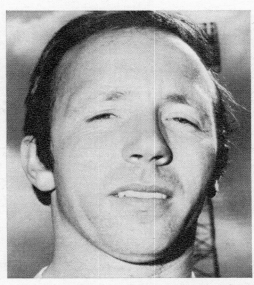

NOBBY STILES (right) and WILF McGUINNESS (below).

all times and first gaining her respect. But although most fathers are keen enough for their lads to become Soccer players, it is usually Mum who makes the final decision.

This is chiefly because she is the one who has an eye, not only on her son's future career, but on his happiness. Once I have convinced a mother that her son will have nice digs, be well looked after, trained only within his own physical limitations, and given the opportunity of further education, or taking a part-time job—I'm well on my way to signing the boy.

And this is not flannel—we do look after young players in this way at Manchester United, for we believe that it not only helps to make them better footballers, but helps build their character.

You may ask why—at my age—I spend my time travelling around the country,

Continued

DENIS VIOLLET (below), another of the ace scout's contributions to United.

THE SUPPLIER OF TALENT

watching schoolboy players, and pitting my wits against other club scouts in my efforts to sign outstanding young players.

It's a long story. For forty-seven years I was a GPO Engineer, and took up full-time scouting only in 1954 when at the age of 60, I retired from the Post Office. Previously, I had been a part-time scout, starting with Manchester City.

It was in the 'twenties when I was running an amateur side in Levenshulme, Manchester, called Cleveland AFC. We won one or two trophies and one of our players, Charlie Needham, signed for Aston Villa who generously gave us a cheque for £35.

When Peter Hodge, manager of Manchester City, heard of this he asked me to do some spare-time scouting for him. And through my association with the City club, I met Matt Busby.

We very quickly became firm friends. That lasted when he was transferred to Liverpool, and through the war years. When after the war he was appointed manager of Manchester United, I joined him on a part-time basis.

And it is really Sir Matt for whom I am now working in a full-time capacity. I wouldn't dream of breaking the partner-ship—and I'm certainly not doing it for the money!

Finally, you might ask for what attributes I am looking when I assess a 14- or 15-year-old boy. Well, first he must have natural ability, for without this, no amount of coaching or training will make him a class player.

Second, I note his physique—not his size—but his build. It is an old but very true saying that if a player is good enough, he's big enough.

This was borne out when, towards the end of last season, Sir Matt was compelled through injuries to play John Fitzpatrick and Nobby Stiles at full-back. Neither of them is a giant, but what a magnificent job they did.

It is very rewarding to me to see "my" lads making the grade in the League side, *but the credit is not all mine*—a lot must go to their shrewd schoolmasters who first note their promise, and to Sir Matt and his trainers and coaches, who bring them along in the right way—at the right pace.

DUNCAN EDWARDS . . . Armstrong was tipped off about him.

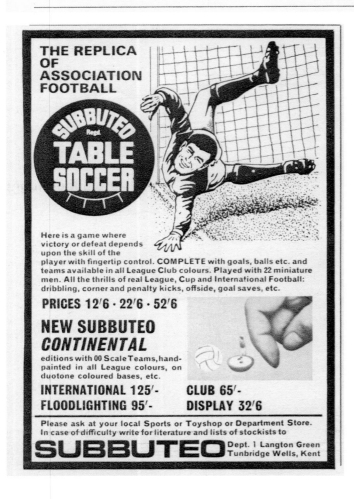

▲ March 1969 | March 1969 | May 1969 ▶

BRIAN
KIDD

Manchester
United

FOOTBALL
MONTHLY

MANCHESTER UNITED

A national image in need of a polish

by PAT COLLINS

THE know-alls, of course, could have told us. More sensible but less pretentious folk might consider that their fears or forecasts have been founded or proved. We could well be saying that it was in the natural order of things, but they wouldn't hear of it for a moment at Old Trafford. . . .

That Manchester United have, or will, run into the sort of lean spell which is the "norm" for so many rivals.

The great difference between United's present wavering fortunes and any other club similarly placed is the club's unique position as the adopted national side.

Leeds, Liverpool, Everton, Spurs, Arsenal, West Ham—they may all falter and flicker and for all the furore within, the ripples would barely extend beyond

▲ November 1969

The Champions. It's May, 1967, and here's Sir Matt holding aloft the Football League trophy while his players applaud.

The current split of a more dedicated, "harder" North to explain Soccer success north of Birmingham was, in the 'thirties, the grudging "Lucky Arsenal" . . . "The Bank of England team" . . . and many other less complimentary terms the further north you went.

Arsenal, even in those so parochial football days, were world-renowned, the pattern for clubs and countries still trying to firmly establish their game.

The general interest and integration brought about by World Cup and European competition was a long way off then. Interest abroad was limited to the top awards of Cup and League. That usually meant Arsenal.

But they never ever endeared themselves to the football public of the 'thirties as United have done in the 'fifties and 'sixties. Nor has any other club in any other period of the game.

The differing background stories of Highbury and Old Trafford and the personalities involved explain it.

Arsenal, to envious rivals, were those jumped-up Southerners who bought success only by cheques . . . for Charles Buchan, David Jack, Alex James, Cliff Bastin and Alf Kirchen among others.

Highbury's marble halls, the club's progressive outlook out-speeding the times, but more—the cool assurance with which they accepted their continued success, only served to feed this envy.

The dash of Lambert, Drake's courage, might be admired, the wiles of James and his long baggy playing pants generated some warmth. But the poker-faced performance of such as Jack, Bastin, Roberts and Hapgood, for all their great ability, seemed to set them—and Arsenal —apart.

In a more personalised and closer-related Press, radio and TV era, we have had the United story unfolding from the "Busby Babes", the emotional upheaval of the Munich crash and the mountain of sympathy, good-will and alliance with the Soccer father-figure of Sir Matt Busby as he has unashamedly laughed and cried with his teams.

All that and the boy-next-door image of Bobby Charlton; the flame and fire of Denis Law; the extrovert entertainment of George Best, the steadfastness of Bill Foulkes along with their many explosive talents and the long, long quest eventually crowned by success in Europe.

There has never been anything at

sporting level to equal the one-night national participation in United's European Cup victory. Even England's World Cup win hardly committed so many so deeply.

Arsenal, Soccer's aristocrats in the entirely masculine following of their hey-day, never had bestowed on them the wide, feminine favour, both matronly and mini-skirted, that is United's.

It has meant a support such as never

Manchester United, under Sir Matt Busby in post-war Soccer, have won five League titles— 1951-2, 1955-6, 1956-7, 1964-5 and 1966-7.

Have been runners-up on seven occasions . . . 1946-7, 1947-8, 1948-9, 1950-1, 1958-9, 1963-4 and 1967-8. They have won the FA Cup twice—1947-8, 1962-3, been runners-up in 1956-7 and 1957-8.

They have won the European Champions' Cup—1967-8—and been semi-finalists in 1956-7, 1957-8, 1965-6, 1967-8 and 1968-9. Their leanest spell was from 1952 to 1955 when they had no direct interest in Cup or League.

In only one other season, 1949-50, were they not directly concerned with the last stages of a League or Cup competition . . . they finished fourth in the League and were knocked out in the Cup's Sixth Round.

---

before. Cold figures alone—that record home League average of 57,549 of 1967-8 and the European Cup win which meant another Football League profit record of £250,000—are still not adequate enough to give the full picture.

No other club have been so generally adopted in these isles. Stop any ten schoolboys ANYWHERE and ask them to name their favourite club. Double check . . . ask their Mums!

It has a basis of many reasons. Not the least being that under Busby their record is unequalled.

Let's hark across to Arsenal again for a moment. They had their run, you can see it here. Since those golden days they have, in the 23 full post-war seasons, won the League title in 1947-8 and 1952-3, won the FA Cup in 1950, were runners-up in 1952 and were runners-up in the last two League Cup Finals.☞

their own local boundaries. But this temporary (?) recession of Bobby Charlton, George Best, Denis Law, Pat Crerand and their team-mates is of national concern, the wondering shared from Camborne to Carlisle, from Colwyn Bay to Chelmsford.

No club have become a national institution as United have since Arsenal in the 'thirties meant English football itself.

There is that parallel between the clubs' scooping of the honours. But whereas Herbert Chapman's Arsenal, imperiously lording it over all, built that great, envious gulf between North and South, United's long reign, checked and then re-charted through the game's most emotion-charged months, has brought a warming regard near to reverence.

Many clubs would like to boast of that record. Arsenal will not. It is sixteen years since they have won anything!

United won nothing last season, are not in Europe this, have made a ragged start and by the time you read this will have played a third of their League games.

They may have climbed nearer respectability and there's STILL the FA Cup to come . . . so why look for red lights already—especially when they have bounced back more than once before?

Arsenal, in the 'thirties, won five League titles—1930-1, 1932-3, 1933-4, 1934-5 and 1937-8 and were runners-up in 1931-2. They won the FA Cup in 1929-30 and 1935-6 and were runners-up in 1931-2.

Like Arsenal, and for far more reason on their modern record, United will not settle for anything less than the best. And the signs have been that another Old Trafford transitional period must be under way before the old arrogance returns to the Stretford Road end.

United may well now throw this right back in my teeth by turning on their full power in chase of the honours, so delighting the hordes who follow them in the flesh and the so many more in the spirit.

It is a measure of their achievements that one could be moved to write in this vein at this stage.

Joe Mercer takes the Cup for Arsenal in 1950. Three seasons later they won the League . . . their last honour.

Floral tribute in July, 1969, in Jersey. A tow and tribute to United winning the European Cup.

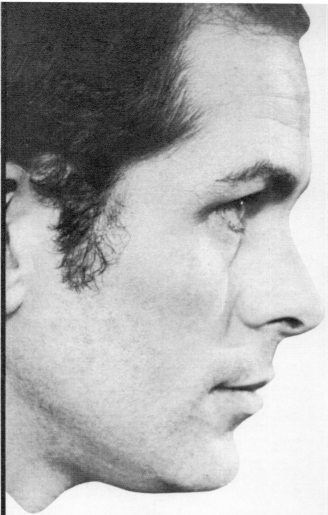

IN THE STEPS OF THE MASTER

Wilf McGuinness tells what it's like to follow Sir Matt Busby

HOW can anyone follow Sir Matt Busby? That, I am well aware, is a question (or comment if you like) that is being bandied around in Soccer circles.

How indeed? He has made the name of Manchester United one to be respected throughout the world. He has established a tradition that even a super-manager would find it difficult to equal, let alone surpass—and has become a legend in his own lifetime!

How then *does* one even attempt to follow him?

This is a difficult question to answer, but the task has been allotted to me—and the ball is well and truly at my feet.

While I have no doubt whatever about the magnitude of my task, I'm not worried about it! It is a tremendous challenge, but I've accepted it, and quite simply I shall get on with the job and do my best.

Sir Matt is still "The Boss!" My title is not team manager but Chief Coach, but it has been made perfectly clear to me that all team matters will be completely under my control.

"The Boss" will (as General Manager) still be there to advise *when called upon*. But I have been given complete freedom of choice so far as team selection is concerned and in the signing or promotion of players, in addition to taking charge of training and coaching.

It is a man-sized job all right, but the only difference from last season so far as I am concerned is the fact that now I have added responsibility.

I am confident (without, I hope, being egotistical) that I will be able to cope—particularly when one views the resources of Manchester United.

We have some of the greatest players in the game, and having been among them for a long time I *know* that they will give me 100 per cent support.

I know that it is often said (as it is of other clubs) that the stars can be difficult, that they don't train as they should.

Don't you believe it! None of them has reached his eminence by slacking, and I know that, for their own sakes as well as for mine, they will work just as hard for me as they did for "The Boss."

We have one of the best appointed training centres—The Cliff—in the game, and no one could wish for better henchmen than Jack Crompton and Johnny Aston.

Fortunately, I have behind me quite a bit of experience in the important aspects of the game. I joined United as an amateur on the same day as Bobby Charlton (there were no apprentices or ground-staff boys then) and apart from Billy Foulkes, I have seen all the present playing staff come into the fold.

At 17, I was stand-in for the great Duncan Edwards at wing-half, I am the proud possessor of a League Championship Medal, played in two European Cup games, have several Under-23 caps, gained a full England Cap at 20 and a second v. Mexico in South America.

It was only a few months after the Mexico match, in a reserve game v. Stoke City (I, along with Harry Gregg, Bobby Charlton and Warren Bradley, had been dropped from the first team) that I broke a leg.

It is now history that the injury was to finish my playing career, but at the age of only 23 I was appointed assistant trainer and have since acted as both trainer and manager to the England Youth side, trainer of England Under-23s, and helped to prepare the England squad for the World Cup in 1966, at Lilleshall, along with Sir Alf Ramsey, Harold Shepherdson and Les Cocker.

So, although I'm the first to admit that I have a lot to learn, I feel that at least I have some qualifications for the important job on hand. It is a top job, and it will not be easy, but I have every confidence that, backed by Sir Matt, the players, and the backroom staff, the glories of Manchester United will continue undiminished.

▲ September 1969

X-RAYON FANS

The Old Trafford scene...

STRETFORD END FANS —AND FANATICS

AND so to Manchester, Old Trafford and the Stretford End mob. My horoscope this particular Saturday morning warned me *"avoid arguments with strangers."* It didn't say carry an umbrella which is what I should have done because it poured solidly all day; heavy, unrelenting Manchester rain.

It cut down United's home gate by some 10,000 without visibly affecting the noisy, singing scarf-waving youngsters in the giant covered Stretford End paddock, packed solid as ever behind the goal.

Let me say that the Stretford End is no true reflection of the Old Trafford crowd when United are home. This is the spot for the cheer leaders, the singers, the chanters and the punch-up youths, all caught up in hysterical non-stop adulation. It is hard to say whether they are there for the singing or the football.

An elderly cloth-capped Mancunian, almost a relic of Meredith's day, was heard to be criticising some slack defensive play by United. In front of me one long-haired fanatic turned to his pal and asked, *"Who's that then, Al Read?"*

The crack was soon forgotten in the chanting for Georgie, Bobby and "the King," Denis Law, who got a hat-trick and took his bows like a poor man's prima donna.

More than 70 per cent. of the Stretford End mob is made up of youngsters between 11 and 18 and they can always be found in the section behind that goal.

There is usually some kind of trouble although on the Saturday I was there it was mild enough—only three policemen needed to pull out a couple of brawling lads.

Like Law, they took several bows, waving grandly to the crowd as they were marched round the track to the tunnel.

As with United supporters in general, the Stretford End youngsters have been rather spoiled by success and now, like our students they are searching desperately for an excuse to demonstrate their militancy.

It is hard to manage this at Old Trafford because they all think alike. It is away from Manchester where the United gangs cause the trouble for there are ready-made enemies on every side.

But this involves the hooligan element you get in every crowd today and I was more interested in specific Old Trafford behaviour at close hand.

Manchester United have a world-wide following, probably no other League club in England can boast so many out-of-town supporters from all walks of life.

I believe only a minority of the average 54,000 Old Trafford crowd really *care* about tactics or team technique and the reason why it is that their team has been the most successful in the post-war period.

The remainder, the hard core fans, are content to leave all that to Sir Matt Busby. They want only to see United win, to recognise the natural skills of stars like Charlton, Law and Best with rapturous applause and to cherish an almost child-like belief that *"we are the greatest"* will sustain for all time.

On almost any Saturday afternoon at Old Trafford or under the brilliant floodlights, watching a United at their best, you could almost believe that.

WE WOULD like to express our feelings about the situation affecting George Best, his club and his country.

George was asked to play four games in eight days, the last game being the World Cup qualifying match against Russia. Surely, George could have been released from the League Cup replay against Burnley on the Monday and allowed to travel with the rest of his colleagues to Russia?

If the match had been a friendly the situation would have been different, but it was not. It was, in fact, one of the most important matches the Irish have ever played. But Manchester United, a club with so much talent available, HAD to play Best in the League Cup, which resulted in injury, and deprived Ireland of the man upon whom they had pinned all their hopes.

Surely this was pure selfishness on the part of United? The League Cup is played every year, but the World Cup every FOUR years.

The blame should be put on United, whose folly in not sacrificing one player, has not only, in our opinion, allowed the wrong team to go to Mexico, but has denied Mexico the chance of seeing the magnificent George Best.

**M. T. GREANEY and
A. JEFFRIES,
99 Berkely Ave., Reading.**

Discipline

PERHAPS MANCHESTER UNITED'S lack of success in the last three seasons can be attributed to lack of discipline on the part of the United management.

Presented with a team of super-stars—George Best, a man who can win matches on his own with the sort of ability only he can produce, Bobby Charlton, the greatest midfield general ever known, Denis—"The King" Law—the United officials, seemingly scared they will lose or displease such stars, have given some of them a totally uninhibited freedom on and off the field.

In my opinion the sloppy, haphazard way of dress of some United players corresponds perfectly to their way of play. And players like Morgan, Best and Fitzpatrick look more like English sheepdogs than footballers.

It is also about time someone realised that half-a-dozen flashes from George Best a season may be thrilling to watch but there are 42 League matches a season.

J. LAMBERT, 276 Leggatts Rise, Watford, Herts.

▲ March 1969

▲ May 1971 | January 1970

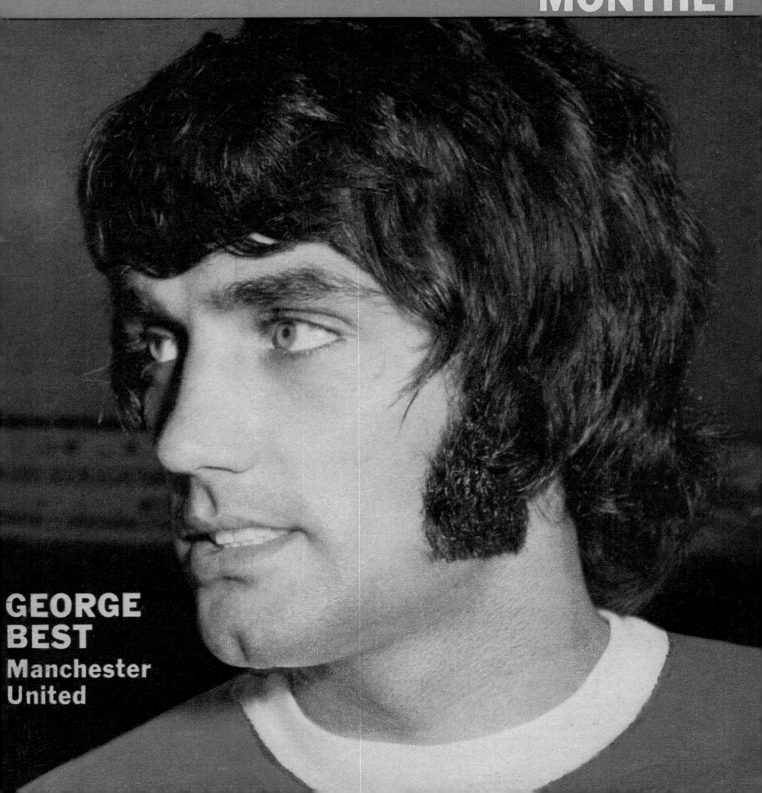

CHARLES BUCHAN'S

FOOTBALL

MONTHLY

APRIL, 1970   THREE SHILLINGS, USA 60 cents

GEORGE BEST
Manchester United

ARE we seeing the end of the reign of Denis "The King" Law? This is the question thousands of Manchester United fans have been asking!

No player in modern times has been given such adulation from his home fans as Denis Law. The Stretford End, the vocal part of Old Trafford, made Law their king a few years ago and even though Georgie Best of the long hair has since burst devastatingly on the scene, it's Law who really still sits on the throne.

For Best is very much the hero of the girls and if you took away the screaming teenage females, Law would still win the loyalty of the boys and youths who make up the bulk of Stretford End support.

Perhaps it is the streak of villainy that ran through Law's early days that appeals to the mob instinct of Stretford Enders. Certainly Law has only to score a goal to re-awaken the crowd's fanatical passion for this controversial, puzzling Scot.

Players like Best and Bobby Charlton are popular of course, especially when they score. But Charlton, sportsman supreme and classical player, and Best who looks more like a pop singer than a footballer, have never really commanded the following of Law, at least from the thousands of male youngsters who swell United's attendances to record level.

The basic reason of course is goals and in this respect Law stands head and shoulders above everyone else at Old Trafford.

Charlton for instance is renowned for his cannonball shot and has scored more goals than any contemporary player at the club. He kicked off this season with a total of 167 League goals, but it had taken him 448 games to score them.

Compare this return with Best and Law. Best at the end of last season had scored 79 times in 213 League appearances . . . but Law has the incredible tally of 140 goals from 226 games.

And in Cup football there just isn't anyone to compare with the Law man. Three years ago he scored his 31st goal in the F.A. Cup to go in front of Stan Mortensen, Ronnie Allen and John Atyeo as the top marksman in post-war Cup Football.

Those goals were scored for Huddersfield Town, Manchester City and, of course, Manchester United. Since then he has scored more goals and beaten Jack Rowley's United club record which stood at 28 goals. For United, Law has a goal-a-game average of 34 from 34 ties, a fantastic record.

In the European Cup he has scored 14 goals for United, one more than Dennis Viollet and another record.

As Law banged in a hat-trick in the first leg against Waterford, the League of Ireland champions, last season and then scored four in the second-leg there was no doubt about who was still king of Old Trafford.

Overall, Law did not have a good 1968-69 season, at least compared with his best years. Yet he still managed to finish up the club's top scorer.

Best was leading marksman in the League with 19 goals, Law next on 14. But whereas Best scored only once in the F.A. Cup and twice in the European Cup, Law netted seven in the English Cup and nine in Europe.

The Law of old we shall never see again. In some respects this is a good thing. The Scot did little to enhance the club's sporting image with two month-long suspensions and one of six weeks—one for kicking an opponent, one for swearing at the referee, and the other for fighting with Ian Ure, now his teammate!

It was his volatile, razor-sharp temperament and it had to be curbed. Law succeeded and has not been in any kind of trouble since his brush with Ure two years ago.

At the same time Law has undoubtedly lost some of the fire and deadly reflexes that made him such a supreme striker.

He was still getting goals last season, as I have said, but they tended to come in comparatively easy matches and not, as in the old days, when the chips were down, the game was in deadlock, and only master footballers could get a goal.

Law of course has also had a fearful battle with injury. He was plagued for a year with a mysterious knee complaint that put him into hospital for an operation when United were winning the European Cup final in May, 1968.

His fans hoped that after feeling his way back to the top of the goal charts last season, he would really become his old formidable self this winter.

But it is clearly not going to be easy. After playing in the first three League games this season he experienced the indignity, along with Charlton, of being dropped. He came back after one game—the first time he had been dropped in his career by the way—only to suffer a further injury to his groin. At the time of writing he had made only 10 appearances, scoring two goals, one in the League Cup semi-final against Manchester City.

Clearly "The King" is not going to be allowed to reign by reputation alone. Chief coach Wilf McGuinness means business as he hurries along in the footsteps of Sir Matt Busby as the team boss.

Manchester United managed to snap out of their worst-ever start to a season without Law's help, and though there is clearly a place for him in the Old Trafford team, he will have to deliver the goods if he is to stay on the throne his fans love so much.

This is Denis the king's testing time.

LAW'S FUTURE?

DAVID MEEK looks at the problem posed by the erratic form of the 'King' of Old Trafford

▲ February 1970

'WHICH OF YOU IS CARLO ?' asked the Boss . . . and that's how

MY CAREER BEGAN—AGAINST ESTUDIANTES!

EVER MET a red-headed Italian ? Well—hello there! One look at me is living proof that not all we Latins are dark-haired and olive-skinned.

Despite my carrot-top and the fair complexion that goes with it I am native-born, of Italian parents, first seeing the light of day at Caderzone in Northern Italy.

But I was only ten months old when my parents brought their family to England and settled in Manchester. When I was old enough I went to school like any other kid—and like the rest, I took to football.

When I first played the competitive game at St. Malachy's School, Collyhurst, Manchester, I was a centre-half, but being on the small side I was eventually moved to the right-wing. Later, when I played for Manchester Boys over two seasons it was in the inside-left position.

By now, I was really bitten by the Soccer bug and wanted nothing better than to be a professional. I had always been a Manchester City supporter and because of my representative appearances, City, West Bromwich Albion, Burnley and others, had made approaches about my future.

In spite of my allegiance to City, I had always looked with envy on the progress to stardom of the famed Busby Babes under Sir Matt Busby—and frankly, I was praying that United would be knocking at the door.

And so it happened! On my very last day at school one of my teachers told me that United's chief discoverer of junior talent, Mr. Joe Armstrong, was coming to see me the very next day.

But I was still rather small, Matt Busby was not sure—and I signed at Old Trafford only as an amateur. For two years I trained two days a week and helped in my brother's business.

I played in the "B" team—the next year in the "A" team—then, when I was 17 and had filled-out a little, I signed professional forms. I was in!

That was in February, 1965. That summer I went to Switzerland with

by
CARLO SARTORI
Manchester United

United's Youth Team and played two games in the Blue Star Youth Tournament. In season 1965-66 I totted-up a dozen appearances in the reserves and played in more than half of the next season's games.

In 1967-68 I was a "regular" in the reserves and in October of the following season the Boss decided to "blood" me on the left wing in a League game against Liverpool at Anfield.

It was no fairy-tale debut (we lost 2-0) but I couldn't have done so badly, for I was one of five substitutes who were on the bench the following Wednesday when United played Estudiantes in the second-leg of the so-called World Club Championship.

After half-an-hour of the first half, Denis Law was injured and came off for attention and that left at least four of the five substitutes (the fifth was goalkeeper Rimmer) wondering which, if any, of us would be called on.

The weather was filthy, we were all sitting there with towels over our heads when Mr. Busby appeared.

"Which of you is Carlo?" he enquired.

"I am," I almost shouted, whipping the towel off my head.

"Get stripped—you're on!" was the Boss's terse instruction.

I was very excited to have the chance of playing in so important a game and this is where I feel my career with United really started.

I began this current season again in the reserves and my big chance really came when Tony Dunne suffered an injury in the League game against Arsenal at Old Trafford.

I had played as substitute for Denis Law again in one match and also had a couple of games at outside right but was not feeling very happy when I was put in against Arsenal. Francis Burns dropped back into Tony's position and I was given his job in midfield. But I managed to score the equaliser, Willie Morgan getting the winning goal.

This was the turning point for having previously played as an attacking inside-forward in the reserves I had at last found my best position in midfield.

But my biggest thrill to date is still the game against Anderlecht in Brussels last season in the European Cup. We had won 3-0 at Old Trafford in the first leg and playing on the left-wing I made it four when I scored my first goal for the senior team eight minutes after the start.

And a good thing I did, too, for we ended up losing 3-1 but took the tie on the 4-3 aggregate. I was a very proud man that night! And in fact I didn't score again for the League side until that goal against Arsenal.

Here's Carlo—ready for a home match with the spaghetti—as mum, Signora Pia Sartori, pours out his native Chianti.

▲ May 1970

IT WAS

Quixall signs for Matt Busby for a record £45,000 fee

In a tussle with City's George Hannah in a Manchester derby

ONE July morning a few years back I was on my way to Old Trafford to cover a county cricket match when I took a wrong turning and pulled up outside a scrap metal merchant's yard and asked for directions.

There was something very familiar about the short, stocky man in his early thirties who smiled pleasantly and then, chuckling, said: "Old Trafford? I reckon you've asked the right bloke. Yes, I think I can manage to get you there."

That shock of fair hair and attractive button face—surely I had seen them before, above the colours of England, Sheffield Wednesday and Manchester United?

"You've got to be Albert Quixall," I said.

"That's me—and I think I am right in saying we stayed in the same hotel in Copenhagen in May 1955," he replied.

Albert Quixall on the scrap-heap—literally. And that was a lot better than being on it metaphorically.

Forced out of football by a knee injury at 32 he had acquired this scrap metal merchant's business near Manchester.

It was odd to think of him selling scrap, this gifted player who ten years before had been weighed in gold when he moved from Wednesday to United at the then record fee of £45,000 and been declared worth £671 an inch.

Before I moved to Fleet Street at the end of 1948 I spent two years with "The Star" at Sheffield and I was already beginning to hear the name Quixall mentioned as a future international although he was still very much the schoolboy.

He came from a modest home on the outskirts of Sheffield, his father being a greenkeeper at Firth Park. Albert, as I recall it, was the eldest of a family of five and during his time at Meynell Road School he was capped for England Boys.

His father said: "Promise me, Albert, you'll join no other club but Wednesday?" Albert promised and it was a happy household when the Owls took him on their groundstaff straight from school.

He came along through the usual channels of Yorkshire League and Central League and developed quickly. In February 1951, at 17, he made his League debut against Chelsea at Hillsborough at inside-right, partner-

ing another 17-year-old, A Finney, also making his appearance.

It was not surprising the should strike up a close frie ship. They went about toge and were known as "Null Void" to the rest of the pla although nobody seems abl remember why.

Another nickname—"Sn —came from an habitual he had at the time and was p ably just a piece of def mechanism at work.

It was always a strain Albert to realise he wa member of one of the coun most famous clubs, working mixing daily with men w names were household word football.

Some of those house words, men like Eric Taylor Alan Brown, thought wel him. They soon discovered things like ball control and tical appreciation came natu to Quixall but at the same the boy had no conceit in and was a careful, respec listener.

They liked, too, the dedic way Quixall and Finney tised their ball skill toge keeping the ball going from to the other literally hundred times without letting it t the ground.

Alan Brown is not the ea man in football to impress Quixall did as a teenager. " didn't have to tell him, he it instinctively. I've seen pull together a line of men had been playing much lo than he had. He just assu leadership."

Albert was a born ga player. Cricket, tennis, minton, table tennis — played them all and rea above-average ability. He one post-war teenager who no problems in adjusting society.

He was apprenticed a joiner, he went swimming dancing and collected Fra Laine and Nat King records.

He won the first of his caps for England in the aut of 1954 against Wales and in space of a year wore the land shirt five times, inclu the tremendous match FIFA at Wembley when land's present team mana Sir Alf Ramsey, scored from penalty spot in the last seconds to make the resul 4-4 draw.

At 21 Quixall seemed to everything life could offe young man and he had by

▲ January 1971

TOUGH AT THE TOP FOR WONDER BOY QUIXALL

says Basil Easterbrook

collected another sobriquet — that of "Fancy Pants".

This came from his habit of hitching up his shorts to a point where, as someone put it, they were "a trifle tight under the arms". Quixall might be said to be the first English footballer to popularise the now universally favoured mini-shorts in these slands.

But now the Quixall story left the realms of the novelette and developed in a way no one had foreseen.

He had won fame with the club he had idolised as a child, the one his father had made him promise to play for if he had the chance, and he had been picked for England.

But in 1955 Quixall lost his place in the England side and Wednesday were relegated to the Second Division.

Wednesday got back at the first time of asking but Quixall did not regain his England status and being a big fish in a comparatively small pool was no longer enough for him.

For the first time the notices were not always kind. The term "prima donna" was used and he was rapped for standing still with hands on hips watching the effect of one sparkling pass.

By the early autumn of 1958 the rumours that Quixall and his once beloved Wednesday were at the parting of the ways grew with a persistence that gave a hollow ring to strenuous denials from Hillsborough that he would never be allowed to leave.

Wednesday went so far as to protest that Quixall had been "got at" and promised dire action, but on September 18, 1958, Quixall signed for Manchester United for £45,000.

It was one of Matt Busby's first moves to rebuild United up to world level after Munich. There was the inevitable handwringing, with all the other First Division clubs agreeing that no single player could be worth £45,000, yet within a few years United thought little about spending nearly a quarter of a million to secure the services of Law, Crerand and Stepney.

Quixall stayed with United for six years all but ten days but could not reach the heights at Old Trafford. For a time his shock of fair hair, his Bikini

shorts and his unquestioned skill gained him plenty of publicity.

But although he had his good games for United he was never the guiding star to restore United's pre-Munich rating that Busby thought he would be. And never again was he picked for England.

When he asked for a transfer United agreed but none of England's First and Second Division clubs showed the slightest interest. For inside-forwards, like bullfighters, the moment of truth comes early in life. In September 1964, at 31, Quixall moved to the other side of Manchester to become a Third Division player with Oldham Athletic. United got back £7,000 of the £45,000 they had laid out for him.

The following evening he found himself down at Dean Court playing against Bournemouth. His association with Oldham was brief and undistinguished. He moved again, another short journey, this time to Stockport County, and the 1966-67 season was to be his last.

Stockport won the championship of the Fourth Division that season but Quixall made only 13 first-team appearances and did not score.

By the beginning of March he was headed for his personal scrapheap out of football with a knee injury. The golden boy who had been the subject of full-page magazine features got a six-line paragraph filling up some odd corner on the sports pages and then—anonymity before 35.

Sports writers do not normally regard scrap metal yards as places likely to produce useful material but I am not sorry I took a wrong turning that day.

Albert Quixall had his years of fame and comparative fortune and I do not believe he wants or needs sympathy, but when I think of him striving for six years to meet the demands made by a club of Manchester United's standing I am aware that "It's tough at the top" is by no means an empty phrase.

Quixall demonstrates his ball control during training at Old Trafford

I'M OUT TO KILL THE 'BAD BOY' IMAGE

NO matter how long I go on playing football — November 28, 1969, is one date that I shall never forget! For it was then I started an eight-week suspension for my misdemeanours on the field.

If you have never played professionally—if you have never suffered in this way—you can have no idea of my feelings at that time. Even now, the mere thought of it hurts like mad.

For several reasons. The loss of money for one, then the frustrating inactivity, allied to the ever-present fear that once reinstated, I might, at the very least, have difficulty in regaining my place in the Manchester United side.

Additionally there was also (on my part) a keen sense of injustice. Not that I have ever made claims to being a lilly-white. Like most humans, I have a temper; I've been known to flare-up in the heat of the moment; I may have been guilty of opening my mouth too wide and too often.

But please believe me when I say very sincerely that never have I deliberately set out to maim an opponent, nor have I wilfully disregarded the rules. Unintentionally perhaps, but never with malicious intent.

I am by nature *aggressive*. It is one of the characteristics that have made me the player that I am. I have always been a 100%, enthusiastic trier—I play it hard. But never, I hope, deliberately dirty.

But rightly or wrongly, I have on more than one occasion crossed referees—and I've paid for it dearly. But you can take it from me that this is all in the past.

I bear no malice—I've learned the hard way but learned I certainly have. To such a degree that nowadays, I take the field with no worries at all so far as my possible behaviour is concerned. I am convinced in my own mind that never again am I going to land myself in serious trouble.

There are several reasons for this. First of all I suppose that I've matured. I now have a wife and a year-old child to support. They require feeding and clothing—I can't afford to be deprived of my pay. And there is also the matter of personal pride. It is my most fervent wish that never again will I suffer the indignity of a suspension.

And there is, too, another important reason. I don't suppose that it has occurred to many, but John Fitzpatrick is the only regular member of the present Manchester United first-team squad *who has never been capped*!

This fact adds fire to my ambition to play for Scotland—and to achieve this I just have to kill the "bad-boy" image. Only the future will prove it—but I'm sure I have at last done just this.

And no one helped me more than Sir Matt Busby. I am well aware that one of my failings was late tackling which got me into a lot of trouble. He took great pains with this problem and had me back at the training ground day after day to iron out the faults.

And the Boss (as he was at the

says JOHN FITZPATRICK
Manchester United

time) showed great faith in me when, at his suggestion, I converted from midfield to my present position at full-back. There was a time when I disliked this position but now, having adjusted to the special requirements, I am thoroughly enjoying my game.

At primary school in my home town of Aberdeen I was usually to be found on the left-wing. Moving on to secondary school I played chiefly at wing-half or inside-forward.

Archie Beatty, who originally discovered Denis Law for Hudderfield Town, spotted me at school and first brought me to Old Trafford to look around before I was 15.

I was impressed, they appeared to like me, but of course I was too young to sign, and went back home to continue playing for Aberdeen Lads Club Thistle, and almost immediately I broke a leg in a cup-tie.

Nine months went by before I was able to kick a ball again—but United hadn't forgotten me. As soon as I was fit I returned to Manchester, and after a two-week trial signed apprentice forms.

I made my Central League debut at 17, and at 18 played my first League game—at left-half in place of Nobby Stiles, who was on Under-23 duty. This was in mid-season, and I played one or two further games before the break.

In the following season I was called upon to deputise not only for Nobby, but for Paddy Crerand and David Sadler, and even appeared in the number seven, nine and ten shirts—but always played a midfield role.

It was after we had played a cup-tie against Watford in January, 1969, that Sir Matt asked me to take the right-back position. I had played at right-half in this game; he told me that he wanted to bring Paddy Crerand back—but wanted to keep me in the side, expressing the opinion that I would do well at the back.

And apart from a few isolated games I have remained there ever since, being lucky enough to regain the position after my lengthy suspension.

Now it is my intention to continue working like mad to hold my position with United—and perhaps one day play for Scotland.

And if I do make it I shall never forget the encouragement and advice given to me by Sir Matt (especially in the troubled times) and by many of my fellow United players, particularly Nobby Stiles, Paddy Crerand, and Denis Law.

Last month's crossword solution

FOOTBALL MONTHLY

WILLIE MORGAN
Manchester Utd

FEBRUARY, 1972   No. 246

Football monthly

FOUNDED IN 1951
BY CHARLES BUCHAN
CAPTAIN OF SUNDERLAND,
ARSENAL AND ENGLAND

EDITOR:
PAT COLLINS

ART EDITOR:
REGINALD BASS

PHOTOGRAPHER:
IAN McLENNAN

ADVERTISEMENT MANAGER:
G. A. IRELAND

YOU MIGHT name several reasons for Manchester United's overdue revival this season. New manager Frank O'Farrell; equally new coach, Malcolm Musgrove; the George Best goals; Bobby Charlton's new lease of life; the midfield industry of Alan Gowling and Willie Morgan . . .

And Denis Law.

That last reason is surprising only if you have an ear to the football ground of Old Trafford. By all the signs Denis Law should not now figure in any part of the Manchester United story.

Two years ago it seemed that Law's career with United, for all the great days together, had reached the point of no return. Two years to this very issue we said almost as much here.

"Law's future?" was the query we posed, and asked in the introduction . . .

"Are we seeing the end of the reign of Denis 'The King' Law? This is the question thousands of Manchester United fans have been asking." Then, in pointing out his long battle to recover from a knee injury, we made the point that ". . . Law has undoubtedly lost some of the fire and deadly reflexes that made him such a supreme striker."

Then was made the comparison between him and other accepted Old Trafford heroes. "Players like Best and Bobby Charlton are popular, of course, especially when they score. But Charlton, sportsman supreme and classical player, and Best who looks more like a pop singer than a footballer, have never really commanded the following of Law, at least from the thousands of male youngsters who swell United's attendances to record level."

Law could well be helping to try to keep Blackpool in the Second Division right now. In fact the story spread in the summer of '70 that he had actually signed for that club.

He was put on the transfer list and United's valuation was then a modest £60,000. Clubs hesitated feeling that if only. . . . But none took the gamble and Denis stayed put.

Any doubts he had about his future, at Old Trafford or anywhere else, he kept to himself. Nagged by injury he didn't make a song and dance about it. We might have been seeing less of that Law trade-mark . . . the raised clenched fist salute to the crowd when he scored . . . but he was making no excuses. He never looked for a wailing wall. His critics could never accuse him of whining, or being a quitter.

Yet even for a player who has made the critics eat their words before, Law's comeback this season has been quite fantastic. His game has mellowed. Still razor-sharp at picking up the chances there is yet a subtle difference in his style. The old flashing arrogance has been re-placed by a quieter, me thoughtful approach.

He turns aside any suggesti that he went about his fight-ba in an "I'll show 'em" mood.

Instead he says: "If there v anything to prove it was myself. You could say that pr comes into it. Apart from a thing else, it was far too early me to go out of the game.

"The whole thing stemm from a knee injury in 1968 . they found this bit of cartila floating about. The next seas the leg was a bit weak. Peo may have thought I was finish . . . but it all boiled down

I FOUND OUT WHO WERE M

▲ February 1972

'THE KING' IS BACK IN BUSINESS

RIENDS says DENIS LAW

fitness.

"I suppose it was partly in the mind as well as physical. But I made up my mind to train right through the close season . . . and it was the best thing that happened, for me. United went to the States and they didn't take me . . . I trained for three months. I trained all through last close season, too, and mentally I felt marvellous; my confidence flooded back."

Did the transfer-listing by United shake him?

"I think I felt a sense of shock about it later on. At the time I wasn't surprised, business is business in football as in anything else.

"I went through a bad two-year spell in my career, and I suppose I was taking my nerves on the field a bit. I still get nervous before every match — Friday nights I don't sleep too well. But now, once I'm on the field, the nerves vanish.

The older, more mellow Denis Law can reflect for a moment to say slowly . . . *"In a way, it's good to reach the bottom as well as hit the top. During my bad spell I found out who were my friends in football as well as outside."*

No longer does he go barging into the 18-yard box "muck or nettles." There's a more calculated air about his forays into the danger zone. He explains: "I weigh up situations more and realise that there's no point dashing in if the end-product isn't going to be there."

But Law remains a specialist in the appreciation of a chance or a half-chance; still the blond bomber keepers fear. Gordon Banks, of Stoke City and England, has long been an opponent—and admirer.

"Denis has done remarkably well for a player who, according to some people, was finished two years ago," says Banks.

"He is an outstanding striker, one of the fastest movers over a short distance, and is constantly looking for mistakes. If a defender slips up Denis is the first to get to the ball. He senses danger and he's in there looking for a goal."

Little about Denis Law has changed, from the Banks point of view. For the keeper, any keeper, he remains a constant menace in the box. "He is just as deadly with head and feet as ever he was," says Gordon.

"Perhaps he doesn't mix it quite the same as far as bodily contact is concerned—but that takes nothing away from his undoubted skill. He can still strike a ball hard, still get up with the best in the area."

And England's keeper echoes the point Law himself made. . . . "He doesn't go chasing from man to man like he used to do. He sizes up situations . . . but he's still in there if the chance is on."

Those close to him will tell you once he accepts you as a friend you will have none better. And if he tells you that his darkest days helped him recognise his real friends you are still left with the feeling that he came through that tunnel in typical Law fashion. . . .

With that steely determination which has always taken him where the action was hottest, as witness the sheer hard graft of his close-season training . . . with the true professional's acceptance that "business is business" and with the manner in which he got back into it.

And above all the realisation that he and he alone could find his way back up the trail.

"There was nothing to prove to people—only to myself."

Denis Law has done it HIS way. . . .

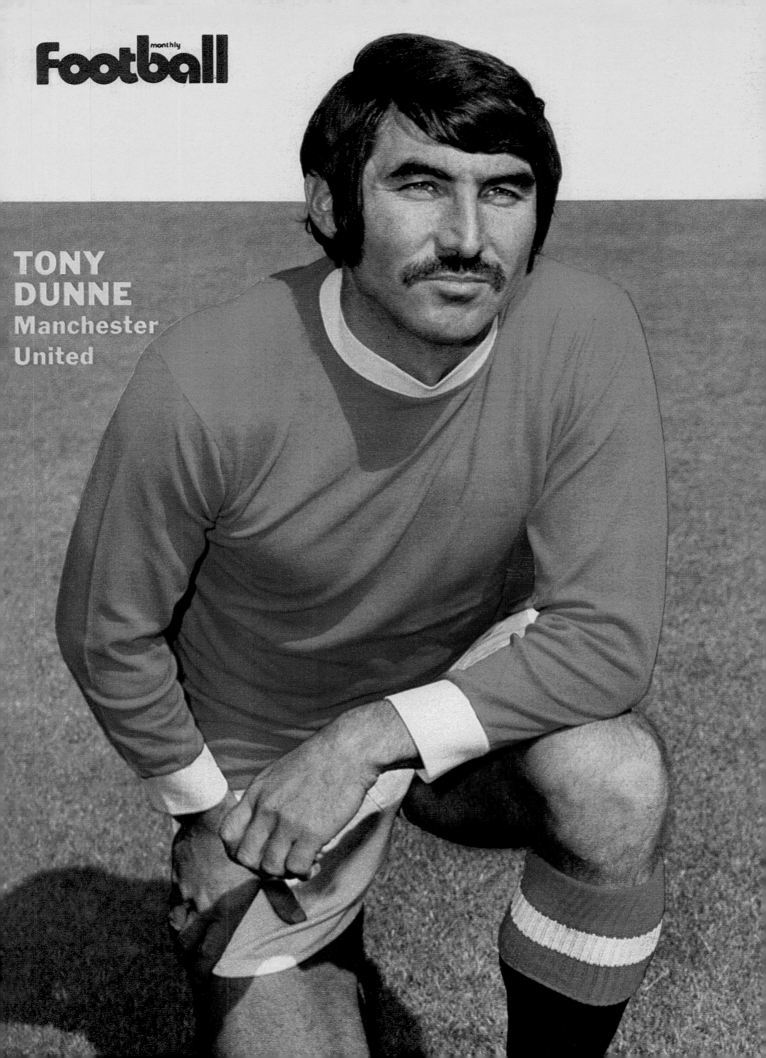

monthly Football

TONY
DUNNE
Manchester
United

DAVID SADLER

Quiet efficiency in the shadow of genius

THE STUNNING resurgence of Manchester United this season, built on the brilliance of Best and Law up front and the invention and industry of Charlton, Morgan and Gowling in midfield, has tended to overshadow the high level of consistency once again shown by kingpin defender David Sadler.

Sadler, an efficient rather than expressive defender, is not the sort of spectacular player who conjures up comparison with his illustrious forwards. By defensive necessity he works quietly and efficiently; plugging holes, tidying up at the back and lending professional expertise to the undoubted potential of talented youngsters like Tommy O'Neill and Steve James.

But his considerable contribution to United's success is an invaluable one in a defence often accused of an inclination to panic under pressure and brittleness at the back.

Yet, without men like Sadler and Tony Dunne—the backbone of the team on days where collective effort is more important than individual flair—the arts of Best and the crafts of Charlton would not be allowed to embellish the United canvas and add that splash of colour that has always characterised their play.

The merits of the man are only conspicuous when he is absent. But Sadler's qualities as a back four defender are fully appreciated by his team-mates, even if he remains one of United's least publicised heroes.

There is much of the traditional English character about Sadler's style; both on and off the field. He is a big, quietly-spoken man whose innate modesty is reflected in his intelligent observations on the game.

He is a player not given to making boastful statements about his individual ability, or the collective merits of the team he plays for. But it is not because of any diffidence on his part, for he is undoubtedly one of the most articulate commentators on the many facets of his chosen profession.

Perhaps his conservative attitude is still tempered by the memory of early days at Old Trafford when he was still in the process of establishing himself in a star-studded side and became the obvious butt of the boo boys.

Yet he talks forgivingly about those painful days when he was treated as United's whipping boy: "It was a difficult time for me," he confesses on reflection. "When I first joined United I was recognised as a front runner. Although I enjoyed playing there I never seemed to get goals when I was in the first team and my confidence suffered.

"I remember not being too happy about my form or my future. There were times when I seemed to be the jack of all trades and master of none. I was playing all over the place—in attack, midfield or defence.

"Frankly, I was just glad to be in the team. But after a while I gradually established myself at left-half in the side and things suddenly changed for me. Basically the difference was that I was now facing the ball and it suited me."

Sadler's steady progress in that position over the next few seasons won him Under-23 and full England honours until he became recognised as a key central

by RAY BRADLEY

DAVID SADLER

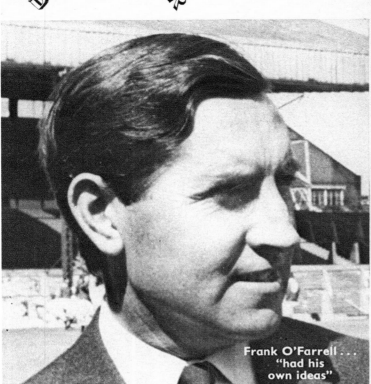

Frank O'Farrell . . .
"had his
own ideas"

Willie Morgan (left) in action
against Wolves' Derek Parkin
—he and Alan Gowling have
given Bobby Charlton a boost

defender.

Today he clearly relishes tha
responsibility and has had muc
to do with the fine progress mad
by Steve James this season.

"Steve has come on tremend
ously," says David, "and wa
just making the position his ow
when he fractured a cheekbone. I
must have come as a terribl
personal blow to him at a tim
when he clearly looked the answe
to United's centre-half problem

"But he has clearly showr
like Tommy O'Neill and Samm
McIlroy that he will figure largel
in United's future. All these boy
are sensible lads who look lik
being very good players indeed.

Of United's critics who claime
that they had "cracked" afte
leading the First Division tabl
for nearly half the season, Sadle
says simply:

"I think they have been ver
unfair. One or two people wh
said we were a "bad" side, sai
only what was to be expected
I suppose it's their way of con
ducting a sort of psychologica
warfare.

"*People in the game have*
right to voice their opinion an
even to criticise others, with th
reservation that they are construc
tive. Tagging us as 'a bad team
hardly seems to me a constructiv
criticism.

"I'm not going to say we're
going to win the championship
or that we haven't played badl
on occasions. But I will tha
the points we accumulated wer

"We are far better going forward . . ." Gowling, Best and Law celebrate a goal against Huddersfield

deserved. We didn't get them by a fluke or because of the benevolence of the opposition.

"When we got to the top we stayed there for almost half a season and that surely proves our success wasn't a fluke.

"Being front runners for so long obviously imposes a strain on you and we felt that pressure when that five-point lead was whittled away.

"We scraped through a few games. Who hasn't? But I'm sure we must stand an equal chance of winning the championship with any team in the top six.

"Of course, it's nice to be top. There is nothing more confidence-boosting than to keep winning. There is no substitute for success. There never will be. But we must learn to live with pressure; just like Leeds have. It's the team that withstands pressure best that carries off the pots."

Even if United fail to carry off the championship this season, Sadler remains convinced that they have now overcome last season's transitional problems and deserve to be bracketed with the top teams in Britain again.

"The credit for our success this season," he says, "must be given to our new manager Frank O'Farrell and coach Malcolm Musgrove. Theirs has been a tremendous joint influence this season.

"Frank and Malcolm came in a blaze of publicity in what was to mark a new era at Old Trafford.

But they came with an open mind. The boss was given infinite advice by a host of outside observers on what United needed to become great again, which players to buy, and so on.

"But he obviously had his own ideas and promised to give everyone a chance. He has kept that promise and we all respect him for it."

If United fans had become disillusioned with lack of success over the past few seasons and it was an open secret that many of Old Trafford's top stars were unsettled by all the chopping and changing last season, plus a revision in accepted style, the appointment of O'Farrell and Musgrove has done much to restore old unity and engender new spirit.

Says Sadler: "Since the boss took over this season we have all sensed a happier environment. As a result the players are happier and this has been reflected by their form."

No-one seems to have benefitted more than Denis Law and Bobby Charlton this season but Sadler refuses to accept, as some have suggested, that their current form has been a direct result of new drive at the top.

"I think Denis is showing all his old fire mainly because he has been free of old injuries," claims David. "He is only doing now what people knew he could always do.

"As for Bobby, he has always

given 100 per cent effort. Bobby will always fight for the ball and work himself to a standstill. Perhaps his fine form this season is attributable to the fact that we now have more strength in midfield.

"With Morgan and Gowling playing so well a lot of the responsibility has been lifted off Bobby's shoulders and has helped him to produce his best form."

Sadler also refutes the suggestion that United's firm commitment to a policy of attacking football this season has left themselves exposed at the back and resulted in a slide after early-season eminence.

"Obviously there have been times when we have been exposed," he claims. "A lot of sides can do this and not get punished. At West Ham we lost 3-0 and people immediately picked on the defence as an excuse for the defeat. But that game was so open it could have ended up 6-5. Yet nobody criticised West Ham's defence.

"If we are to be condemned for being positive that's a different matter. But we play the way we know best. We are far better going forward and we must try to capitalise on our assets and abilities.

"We don't attempt to stifle natural talents and we never will."

On reflection David adds: "It's a peculiar thing being a United player. Everyone seems to want to

beat us. All our matches seem to be a quality test for the opposition. Every game seems to be played at Cup-tie pressure.

"When I first joined the club I found it difficult to understand why we should be singled out. Now I've grown to accept it—just as everyone else accepts it. Perhaps it's a compliment to our ability."

On a more personal note Sadler also accepts that his international future, at 26, must be governed by the form of Bobby Moore.

"There's not much chance of dislodging Bobby Moore," he says, "so you have to be realistic about it. I've won four full caps for England but they were all at centre-half.

"Now I'd be happy just to get back into the squad. I loved playing for England at all levels. It was marvellous—the ultimate ambition for any footballer. But now I tend to think that most of my future ambitions centre on Manchester United."

Such a realistic appraisal of his own talents and limitations make the modest manner of David Sadler a positive virtue, and a credit to the profession he has served so well.

NEXT MONTH
Don't miss our April issue and the result of our great F.A. Cup competition.

Like his idol, George Best, Manchester United's new Irish signing Trevor Anderson, is popular with the girls. But Ann Beattie and Yvonne King are two of the girls he left behind when he went to Old Trafford

United should get best of this bargain

AMIDST the plethora of £200,000 transfers recently the ordinary follower of the game could be excused if he did not notice a deal involving Manchester United and the Irish League club, Portadown.

It was modest by United standards—a mere £20,000 was involved.

Not much when you think of the astronomical sums now being paid, but let me quote the words of United manager Frank O'Farrell: "This could prove to be a wonderful investment for a small outlay."

Most Soccer afficinadioes in Northern Ireland would agree, for United's latest Irish capture, 21-year-old striker Trevor Anderson is rated one of the most outstanding prospects in the last 20 years.

His ambition was to be a professional footballer. His favourite club — Manchester United. And his idol—George Best.

Often Trevor was called "Georgie" by his team-mates. Not only was he a member of Cregagh Boys Club, in which Best was discovered, but he physically resembles him, too.

The build is the same; the body swerve, the fantastic ability to screen a ball, the lethal shot in either foot and the tremendous acceleration over the first 20 yards. He has poise and assurance—indeed all the attributes.

Huddersfield Town offered him a trial when only 15, but on the scene stepped Portadown manager Gibby MacKenzie, who took one look at the player and immediately recognised his potential.

"The Gibb" is too shrewed in the ways of football to let such a gem slip through his hands.

He developed Anderson in an almost imperceptible fashion. And then, 18 months ago, let him burst into the Irish League; his arrival had the impact of a thunderbolt as everybody sat up and took notice of the new boy.

This applied particularly to the talent spotters of English and Scottish clubs who honeycomb Ulster and find it quite a lucrative area despite the civil tension and unrest. The number of players still being signed up is phenominal.

MacKenzie sang Anderson's praises to many cross-Channel clubs. He wanted the boy to get on; his team to benefit with some cash and to give other young hopefuls struggling through the present crisis an incentive to play well and, perhaps, follow suit.

The queue of those making inquiries became like a Who's Who of football. They came, watched but, strangely, never made a bid. Not even Manchester City, whom Gibby represents in Ireland as well as holding down his Portadown managerial post.

A personal letter to the manager of one Scottish club went unanswered. But MacKenzie, the red-headed Scot with the fanatical zeal, never gave up.

Then he telephoned United and had a quick word with O'Farrell and the deal was settled.

At last his recommendation had been accepted. O'Farrell relied on the MacKenzie judgment and that of the discerning Northern Ireland Soccer public.

It was Anderson, born almost within the shadows of Windsor Park, Belfast, who inspired the club during the last two seasons to end a 19-year run without a trophy.

And it was Anderson who helped raise the gates to a record level, quite an achievement these days.

He is the most naturally gifted player ever handled by MacKenzie, who has sent quite a few players to cross-Channel clubs.

They include **Dave Clements** (Sheffield Wednesday); **Errol McNally** (Chelsea); **Harry Robinson** (Fulham); **Billy McCullough** and **Jimmy Magill** (Arsenal); and **Tommy Herron** (Manchester United).

O'Farrell, now attempting to improve the off-field image of his players, asked Anderson to have his hair cut before reporting at Old Trafford. "I had this done immediately. Long hair means nothing when you are given a chance like this," says Trevor.

Now he is concentrating on becoming a true professional, getting superbly fit, playing himself into the top grade and eventually, I forecast, winning a Northern Ireland "cap".

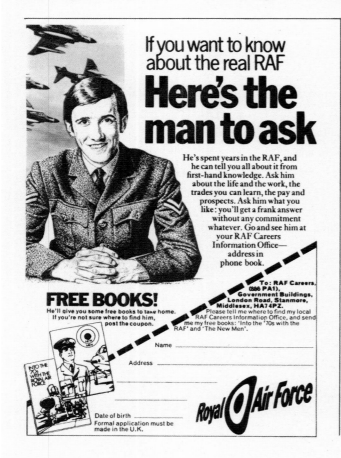

MARTIN BUCHAN
Manchester United

‘I take the decisions . . . and I stand or fall by them’

THE thing to remember is that it's just a football club; just like Coventry or Leicester or Crystal Palace. It gets a couple of points and makes a lot of money when it wins, but if it keeps on losing matches then it'll be relegated in which case they'll sell half the players and probably sack the manager.

Just a football club. Remember that.

You remember it, in fact, all the way to the front door with the "United Crisis" headlines tucked under your arm and a string of fiercely probing questions for the manager in your head.

Then you see the memorial to the men who died at Munich fourteen years ago; you walk through to the lounge where the trophy cases bulge with evidence of fifty years of unimaginable success and you stare out at the empty terraces (did they really get 52,000 in last Saturday?) and the resolution dissolves.

It is not just a football club. It is not like Coventry or Leicester, nothing like Crystal Palace. It is **Manchester United** and the fellow in charge of it has had more than enough of everyone's questions, probing or otherwise.

"The things some of them are saying about me! Honestly, you'd have to be a real hard case not to get upset by some of them," says Frank O'Farrell.

"People I've known for a long while are starting to scream about how badly I've bought and how the job's proving too big for me. And I read the stuff and think 'What have I ever done to you? Why are you writing me off without giving me a decent chance?' I know it's silly to let it get through to you, but it does.

"You see, this is the job I've always wanted; it's the job everyone in football wants. But I didn't want it because it was easy. They don't pay you this kind of salary for doing something that's easy.

"I think it's the most difficult job in football. There isn't a manager in the game who experiences the same pressures as the manager of Manchester United.

"It isn't just the traditions of the club or the fact that you're following a great man like Matt, it's this emotional thing the club has built up with the public.

"United is everyone's second

JANUARY, 1973 No. 257

FOUNDED IN 1951
BY CHARLES BUCHAN
CAPTAIN OF SUNDERLAND,
ARSENAL AND ENGLAND

EDITOR:
PAT COLLINS

ART EDITOR:
REGINALD BASS

PHOTOGRAPHER:
IAN McLENNAN

ADVERTISEMENT MANAGER:
G. A. IRELAND

Cover-Pic: Spurs v. Stoke at White Hart Lane

▲ January 1973

FRANK O'FARRELL

The man with the most glamorous—and most difficult—job in football talks about it to John Anthony

love. You look for the result of your own team, then you look for United's result. The interest is ridiculous.

"Look, I left Bobby Charlton out of the side. Fair enough, I expected some reaction with a player as popular as Bobby involved. But the letters I got!

"They came from all over the world! And all telling me I was wrong. That's when you realise how many people are looking at you, when you get a reaction like that."

It would be wrong to suggest that this season of trial has inflicted any visible scars on O'Farrell. Encased in pin-stripes and breaking off sentences to cope with a constantly buzzing inter-com, he looks like nothing more than the rising young executive who's seriously thinking about cutting out bread and potatoes.

He encourages the image up to a point: "I don't lose sleep over our troubles," he says. "I went through the insomnia thing years ago when I was at Weymouth and we were near the bottom of the Southern League.

"We got out of trouble pretty well in the end; things turned for us and I learned how to evaluate situations. That experience has helped me a lot this time."

But the pressures are now vastly different. There was no Busby to emulate, no Best to accommodate at Weymouth. O'Farrell reasons it out:

"There were problems when I came here. Of course there were, otherwise I wouldn't be here.

"*But I want to make it clear that the problems were not Busby problems. I've had nothing but help from that man all the time I've been at Old Trafford.*

"It's something the mischief-makers can't understand. Some are saying that I'm under his thumb, which is rubbish. **I take the decisions just like any manager has to. And I stand or fall by them.**

"But others are saying that I disregard him, that I've no respect for the man. Now honestly, how could you be in football and not respect him?

"He's seen it all. Everything's written in his face, isn't it? I knew all about his career, like everyone else, when I came here. But I've only recently realised what it all meant.

"We were away to Sheffield United some time ago. We played well and it looked like we'd get a draw until the very last minute when Currie or

Ted MacDougall . . . a costly
capture from Bournemouth

someone hit a great shot that looked as if it was going inside our post. Then suddenly it swerved and stayed out and I think I screamed with relief.

"Matt was sitting next to me and I said to him: 'How the bloody hell did you put up with this for twenty-five years?' And he laughed!

"But it's a thought, isn't it? I mean, how many of those situations has he experienced? And how often has he seen the ball go in instead of staying out? Incredible man."

Skill alone is not enough to become a part of the new United which O'Farrell is in process of building. It is a United which will bear little or no resemblance to the side which disguised a multitude of faults by winning the European Cup in 1968.

Names like Charlton, Law and, probably, Kidd, will have left the scene when the new side is formed and one of the new stars will be the man whom £220,000 brought from Bournemouth.

"We had more than 50,000

Ian Moore . . . he will do
for O'Farrell

here to see Ted MacDougall's first home match," says O'Farrell. "I said to him: 'They're waiting to crown new kings out there. Get out and take the chance'."

It is the kind of vivid phrase which O'Farrell, unlike the average Cork man, rarely allows himself, but it adequately conveys his aspirations for MacDougall.

"He'll do me," he says. "And so will Martin Buchan, Ian Moore and Wyn Davies. All right, so they cost around £600,000 altogether. If they can give our crowd the success it deserves, they'll have been cheap at the price.

"Of course, some people resent the spending. Tony Waddington, I believe, was pretty scathing about clubs like United splashing out £200,000 on a player. He said it was inflationary.

"What he didn't say was that Stoke charged Everton £140,000 for Mike Bernard last season. I'm sure Harry Catterick would have been delighted to have got him for half that figure, but that's what Waddington charged.

"Inflation works both ways, you see. You either get involved in buying the best or you keep out and say the market's mad."

Whatever happens, you may be sure that Manchester United will not keep out of the buying line while there is still a team to be built. They will buy and blend and trust that unlimited sweat and a proud tradition will see them through the present crisis.

The future is in the hands of Frank O'Farrell.

They took a long while choosing him and they did not choose lightly, for they realised there are lots of people around with the ability to run a football club.

Manchester United is different.

The European Cup success of 1968
that papered the cracks

Busby welcomes O'Farrell
to Old Trafford . . .
"I have had nothing
but help from
Sir Matt"

Number nine, R. Charlton, Manchester United and England, waves his last farewell to League football. A sad day at the end of a wonderful career

▲ 1974 Gift Book

Postscript

When 35 year old Bobby Charlton bowed out in 1973 after a record 759 appearances for United, for all his stature in the game, he had no cause for complacency.

Indeed compared with today's United players, most of whom should be financially comfortable for the rest of their lives, it is worth remembering that the majority of stars who featured on the pages of *Charles Buchan's Football Monthly* faced more uncertain prospects.

Munich survivor Albert Scanlon, for example, ended up playing for Lincoln and Mansfield. Struggling to clear his debts, he later worked in a bakery, a factory, a warehouse and then as a security guard.

Team-mate Johnny Berry never played again after Munich and set up a sports shop, before working in a Radio Rentals warehouse. Jackie Blanchflower, 24 when the disaster ended his career, drifted from job to job, as a newsagent, bookmaker, publican and later, in accountancy. Before his death in 1998 at the age of 65 he also discovered a talent as an after dinner speaker.

Stan Pearson became a sub-postmaster. Mark Pearson went into engineering in Bradford. Albert Quixall set up a scrap metal business in Manchester, only to fall on hard times and be helped out by a benefit match.

Of the 1968 team, John Aston opened a pet shop in Stalybridge, while Tony Dunne ran a golf driving range in Altrincham.

John Fitzpatrick, his career cut short at the age of 26, set up a wine import business in Aberdeen, while Carlo Sartori, after enjoying a modest career with various Italian clubs, started a knife sharpening business for Manchester hotels.

No doubt inspired by Messrs Busby and Murphy, a comparatively large number of former Reds went into management.

Allenby Chilton went to manage Grimsby Town in 1955. He later ran a pub, then managed non-League Wigan and Hartlepool. Thereafter he ran a shop, before completing 14 years in a steelworks.

Jack Rowley spent five years as manager at Plymouth, followed by a series of appointments, including one season at Ajax of Amsterdam, in 1963-64. He finally left the game in 1969 and ran a sub post office in Oldham.

After leaving United in 1953, Johnny Carey led Blackburn to the First Division before moving to Everton, where he engineered their highest placing since the war, only to be sacked by chairman John Moores, the head of Littlewoods, in the back of a London taxi. Carey then steered Leyton Orient to Division One, before further spells at Nottingham Forest and Blackburn. He later worked for a tile company and in the treasurer's office of Trafford Borough Council, down the road from Old Trafford.

Bill Foulkes stayed on at Old Trafford for five years to hone his coaching skills before managing clubs in Chicago, Tulsa and San Jose, followed by eight years in Norway and three years in Hiroshima. Finding himself short of funds, in 1992 Foulkes auctioned mementoes from his playing career at Christie's. His 1968 European Cup medal sold for £11,000.

Ray Wood, who played only one further match for United after Munich, travelled even further, coaching in Canada, Zambia, the USA, Ireland, Cyprus, Greece, Kuwait, Kenya and the United Arab Emirates, before returning in the 1980s to run a sports shop in Bexhill. His last job was in a Hastings department store.

Dennis Viollet also tried coaching, with Witton, Linfield (in Belfast) and Preston, then management with Crewe. From there he moved

to coach in Jacksonville, Florida, where he died in 1999, aged 65. The Dennis Viollet Memorial Cup is now contested every year by university teams.

In common with most clubs, United have often found employment for former players. Jack Crompton left his coaching post at Luton to help out after the Munich disaster, and stayed on until 1971. He then worked at Barrow, Bury and Preston before returning for a third spell at Old Trafford as reserve team coach.

Fellow goalkeeper Harry Gregg also coached at United for a period, in between managerial spells at Shrewsbury, Swansea, Crewe, Swindon and Carlisle. Awarded an MBE in 1995, Gregg was always remembered as one of the heroes of Munich, having hauled several passengers from the burning wreck. But he was also the most vociferous in his criticism of United for their treatment of the survivors.

Ian Greaves, who missed that fateful trip with an injury, also managed, at Huddersfield, Bolton, Oxford, Wolves and Mansfield, while Trevor Anderson, after failing to live up to his billing as the new George Best, took up management in his native Northern Ireland with Linfield, Newry, Ards and Dundalk.

Less successful were Martin Buchan, who lasted four months in the Burnley hotseat and is now an official at the Manchester-based Professional Footballers Association, and Nobby Stiles, first in post at Preston, then at West Bromwich Albion, where he teamed up with his brother-in-law, Johnny Giles. (Now a leading football analyst in the Irish media, Giles is one of the few players whose career actually improved after leaving United, being best remembered as part of Don Revie's mighty Leeds team.)

After the Hawthorns, Stiles returned to United to help coach the

youth team. For his part in winning the 1966 World Cup he was also awarded an MBE in 2000.

Another Old Trafford returnee was Wilf McGuinness. Following his traumatic departure in 1971 McGuinness coached in Greece, before managerial spells with York, Hull and Bury. Today, in common with Stiles and former goalkeeper Alex Stepney, he is an after dinner speaker, and also a match day host at Old Trafford.

Also to be seen at Old Trafford on a regular basis are Pat Crerand, a commentator on the club's MUTV channel, and David Sadler, who contributes articles on the club to the local media. Crerand and Sadler, together with Warren Bradley (see right) and Busby Babe John Doherty were also instrumental in establishing the Manchester United Former Players Association.

Of all the players to return to Old Trafford none had a greater impact than Collyhurst-born Brian Kidd.

After leaving United Kidd went on to enjoy a successful scoring record with Arsenal, Manchester City, Everton and Bolton, before finishing his career in the North American Soccer League. He then served his managerial apprenticeship with Swindon, Preston and Barrow, returning to United as part of their pioneering Football in the Community scheme in 1988.

Working his way up the coaching ladder under Alex Ferguson, Kidd's presence played a key part in helping United to the Premier League title in 1993. Indeed the Reds went on to win another three Premier League titles and two FA Cups before Kidd decided to return to management in his own right with Blackburn in December 1998. But the transition did not suit him, and he resumed a supporting role, first as part of the England set up, then with Leeds and, more recently, at Sheffield United.

Schoolteacher Warren Bradley (*right*) was an amateur with Bishop Auckland when he agreed to help out United after the Munich disaster. He later became a head teacher and school inspector, while helping to run United's former players' association. Bradley, who uniquely played for England at both full and amateur level in the same season, died in 2007, aged 73. Shay Brennan (*far right*) was the first United player to receive a pension from the club. He ran a parcel courier business in Waterford before his death on a golf course in 2000, aged 63.

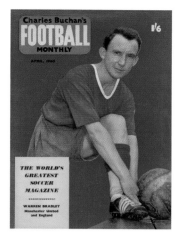

And what of the three great legends who played alongside Kidd in the 1968 European Cup?

Such is Bobby Charlton's renown – it was once said that he was even more famous abroad than the Queen – that readers will hardly need reminding of his post-United career. After that farewell game in 1973 Charlton became player-manager at Preston, with Nobby Stiles as his coach. But he too proved unsuited to management, and after returning as a player at Waterford, and later in South Africa, Charlton became a director at Wigan and concentrated thereafter on building a business and media career. Among his successes is the *Bobby Charlton Soccer and Sports Academy*, which runs youth schemes around the world and numbers amongst its alumni a 12 year old called David Beckham.

Awarded a CBE in 1974, Charlton joined the United board in 1984 and ten years later was knighted. In a wider role he has acted as ambassador for the city of Manchester, in its various bids for the Olympic and Commonwealth Games, and for the FA when bidding for the 2006 World Cup.

Approaching his 70th year as this Gift Book went to press, Charlton remains on the board at Old Trafford, one of the most respected elder statesmen in world football.

Released by United in 1973, Denis Law moved back to his former club, Manchester City. A year later his last ever act in an English domestic game was to back heel a goal through Alex Stepney's legs in a match which confirmed United's relegation to Division Two. Although the Reds would have gone down anyway, Law was so upset that he asked to be substituted immediately, as United fans invaded the pitch in a vain attempt to have the match abandoned.

Law subsequently built a successful career as a media pundit, and remains in close touch with United, where his daughter works in the press office. Known to Reds fans as 'The King', Law is also commemorated by a bronze statue on the upper deck of the Stretford End, unveiled in 2002.

For George Best his sacking by United in 1972 was the start of a peripatetic career. After spells at Dunstable Town, a few matches in South Africa and with Stockport County, he found some stability with Fulham and in North American soccer. By the 1980s he was finishing his League career with Bournemouth before making guest appearances for clubs as diverse as Scone Thistle, Glentoran and Nuneaton Borough, as he struggled to cope with bankruptcy, a jail sentence for drink driving and a steady, and very public descent into alcoholism. His eventual death in November 2005, at the age of 59, was marked by unprecedented media coverage. An estimated 100,000 mourners turned out for his funeral in Belfast.

Despite his wild reputation, a year later Belfast Airport was renamed in Best's honour, while the Ulster Bank issued a five pound note bearing his portrait, thereby unleashing a frantic sale amongst fans and collectors.

At Old Trafford Best will also be commemorated by a new statue, this one featuring the 'Holy Trinity' of Best, Charlton and Law. This work is due to be placed under the watchful gaze of another statue, that of Sir Matt Busby (sculpted by Philip Jackson), which sits regally on a pedestal outside the East Stand, facing what used to be Warwick Road but has been known since 1993 as Sir Matt Busby Way.

After retiring in 1971 Busby served both as a director of the club and as a member of the Football League's Management Committee (ironic, given the clash of wills between Busby and the League over Europe in 1957). In 1982 he was elected Vice-President of the League, and subsequently President of United. For one season after his death in 1994, at the age of 84, his seat in the South Stand was left vacant, tied with a black ribbon.

In recent years the game of football has often been accused of over-sentimentalism. Numerous stands have been named after individuals, in the continental style. Statues of former heroes have sprung up outside stadiums, while the wearing of black armbands and the observation of a minute's silence, or increasingly a minute's applause, have become ever more commonplace following the passing of a former player or manager.

Yet such displays of respect must surely be better than the almost callous disregard for history which previously prevailed.

Even the victims of Munich are better commemorated now than they were at any time in the immediate decades which followed.

At Old Trafford itself there are two memorials. One is a clock, donated shortly after the disaster by United's Ground Committee of stewards and gatemen. (Contrary to popular belief it is not stopped at 3.04 pm, the time of the crash.) The other is a handsome plaque, a copy of one put up in the early 1960s, listing the victims, players and officials.

A third memorial, in the form of a walkway, is also planned, to mark the disaster's 50th anniversary in 2008. In Munich there is a further memorial, recently improved, close to the crash site.

Of the victims, Duncan Edwards is by far the most lauded, although the current scale of commemoration is also a recent phenomenon.

Edwards' home town of Dudley was quick to honour his career with stained glass windows at St. Francis' church, featured on page 65. But only in 1999 was a more public memorial erected, in the form of a statue in the town's market place. A permanent display of his memorabilia is also scheduled to appear at Dudley Museum and Art Gallery.

Still in Dudley a street, a public house and a sports complex have been named after Edwards, as have the local council's sporting awards. His grave in Dudley cemetery is also a shrine, regularly bedecked with floral tributes by visiting fans.

Back in Manchester, in Newton Heath, birthplace of United, there are also sheltered homes known as Duncan Edwards Court.

In the same vicinity, off Millwright Street, are streets named after three other Munich victims, Roger Byrne, Tommy Taylor and Eddie Colman. There are also student flats at Salford University named after Colman, on Belvedere Road.

But compared with the memorials to Edwards, these appear as only token tributes, particularly in the case of Gorton-born Byrne, who played such an influential role in the club's post war development.

At the same time fellow Munich victims Mark Jones, David Pegg and Geoff Bent have been barely remembered at all, while only recently has Bill Whelan been honoured, by having a bridge named after him in Dublin.

However all the victims of the disaster are fully commemorated in Manchester United's museum, a museum which, when set up in 1986, was the first of its kind in British football.

Compared with other branches of mainstream popular culture, football has been relatively late in taking steps to protect its heritage. At Old Trafford, and amongst United's legions of followers, that process remains a work in progress.

Index

Further reading

Adamson, Richard *Bogota Bandit: the Outlaw Life of Charlie Mitten, Penalty King of Old Trafford* Mainstream (1996)
Best, George *Blessed: The Autobiography* Ebury Press (2002)
Best, George *Hard Tackles and Dirty Baths: the Inside Story of Football's Golden Era* Ebury Press (2005)
Burn, Gordon *Best and Edwards* Faber & Faber (2006)
Busby, Matt *Matt Busby's Manchester United Scrapbook* Souvenir Press (1980)
Busby, Matt and Jack, David *My Story* Souvenir Press (1958)
Cantwell, Noel *United We Stand* Stanley Paul (1965)
Charlton, Bobby *My Manchester United Years* Headline (2007)
Connor, Jeff *The Lost Babes: Manchester United and the Forgotten Victims of Munich* Harper Sport (2007)
Crerand, Paddy *Never Turn the Other Cheek* Harper Sport (2007)
Crick, Michael and Smith, David *Manchester United – Betrayal of a Legend* Pelham (1989)
Doherty, John and Ponting, Ivan *The Insider's Guide To Manchester United* Empire Books (2005)
Dunphy, Eamon *A Strange Kind of Glory: Sir Matt Busby and Manchester United* Heinemann (1991)
Edwards, Duncan *Tackle Soccer This Way* Stanley Paul (1959)
Foulkes, Bill and Wright, Ben *Back at the Top* Pelham (1965)
Gowling, Alan *Football Inside Out* Souvenir Press (1977)
Green, Geoffrey *There's Only One United* Hodder and Stoughton (1978)
Gregg, Harry and Anderson, Roger *Harry's Game: an Autobiography* Mainstream (2002)
Hughes, Brian *Star Maker – the Untold Story of Jimmy Murphy* Empire (2002)
Hughes, Brian *The Smiling Executioner – The Tommy Taylor Story* Empire (1996)
Hughes, Brian and Cavanagh, Roy *Viollet – the Life of a Legendary Goalscorer* Empire (2001)
Inglis, Simon (ed) *The Best of Charles Buchan's Football Monthly* English Heritage (2006)
Kennedy, John *Tommy Taylor of Manchester United and Barnsley: Busby Babe* Yore Publications (1994)
Law, Denis *The King – Denis Law, the Autobiography* Bantam (2003)
McCartney, Iain *Roger Byrne – Captain of the Busby Babes* Empire (2000)
McCartney, Iain and Cavanagh, Roy *Duncan Edwards – a Biography* Temple (1988)
McGuinness, Wilf *Man and Babe: the Autobiography of Wilf McGuinness* Parrs Wood Press (2006)
Meek, David *Heroes of the Busby Era* Orion (2007)
Meek, David *Red Devils in Europe – the Complete History of Manchester United in European Competition* Hutchinson Radius (1990)
Murphy, Jimmy and Taylor, Frank *Matt, United and Me* Souvenir Press (1968)
Parkinson, Michael *Best – an Intimate Biography* Hutchinson (1975)
Roberts, John *The Team That Wouldn't Die* Arthur Barker (1975)
Stepney, Alex *Alex Stepney* Arthur Barker (1978)
Stiles, Nobby *After the Ball: My Autobiography* Hodder & Stoughton (2003)
Taylor, Frank *The Day a Team Died* Souvenir Press (1983)
The Official Manchester United Illustrated History Carlton (2001)
Whelan, Tony *The Birth of the Babes: Manchester United Youth Policy, 1950-57* Empire (2005)
Williamson, Stanley *Munich Air Disaster – Captain Thain's Ordeal* Cassirer (1972)

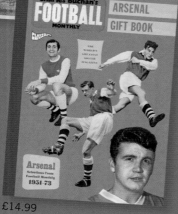
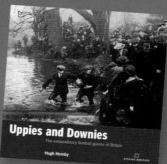